WAKING UP IN THE SPIRITUAL AGE

Dr. Dan Bird

For permission, serialization, condensation, adaptions, or for our catalog of other publications, write to Ozark Mountain Publishing, Inc., P.O. box 754, Huntsville, AR 72740, ATTN: Permissions Department.

Library of Congress Cataloging-in-Publication Data

Bird, Dan – 1952 -

Waking Up In The Spiritual Age by Dr. Dan Bird

A major Spiritual shift is occurring in this world, and more people are experiencing unexpected phenomenon in their daily lives.

This book is for those who are experiencing this shift but are not sure of what they are feeling. It is an introduction of sorts for "newly awakening" individuals who feel there is more to life than we are aware of using our five senses. What if those intuitive thoughts and dreams are messages? What is their purpose? I believe they can help us make sense of why we are here, and guide us to reach our highest potential and goals. This help is available to everyone, but only if we are aware of it. Spiritual help is all around us.

If you are ready to begin your own Spiritual journey, this book is for you!

1. Metaphysical 2. Spiritual Shift 3. Manifestation 4. Meditation

I. Bird, Dan, 1952- II. Metaphysical III. Manifestation IV. Title

Library of Congress Catalog Card Number: 2016930415

ISBN: 9781940265339

Cover Art and Layout: www.noir33.com

Book set in: Lucida Fax, Ringbearer

Book Design: Tab Pillar

Published by:

PO Box 754, Huntsville, AR 72740

800-935-0045 or 479-738-2348; fax 479-738-2448

WWW.OZARKMT.COM

Printed in the United States of America

TO MY MOTHER, BETTY LOU BIRD, WHO HAS ALWAYS
SHOWN US HOW IT IS DONE.

ENDORSEMENTS

"*Waking Up in the Spiritual Age* is truly a gift to behold...written directly from the Soul. For all of us who've been touched by the unseen world in one way or another, Dr. Dan not only validates the experiences we've had, but also inspires us to continue our quest of remembering who we really are as spirits having a human experience."

~ Angela Pennisi, Medium and Intuitive Teacher at
SoulWorks.com

"Dr. Dan Bird's book is the answer to the painful question that so many of us ask when we begin our spiritual journey, "What is happening to me?" Whether you're willingly or stubbornly moving down a spiritual path, this book is the perfect grounded field guide to navigate the "growth-inducing downs" and the "awe-inspiring ups" of awakening. I can't wait to see what Dan is guided to give us next."

~ Deb Brockmann - Life Coach and Author of
Before the Secret - Interview with the Other Side

"Authenticity prevails! An unique voyage of awakening that is straight forward, written beautifully, and surrounds the reader with truth and grace."

~ Ms. Patty, Spiritual Channel at Soul Echoes

"*Waking Up in the Spiritual Age*" is a great read for those who are trying to understand their newly awakened spiritual selves. Dan writes from the heart in an easy to understand way, and shares his own personal experiences with the reader. I would definitely recommend this book!

~ Gina Hickcox, Intuitive Healer @HealingbyGina.com

TABLE OF CONTENTS

Chapter 1

Introduction, Or How I Found Myself

This book is intended for those folks who find themselves just waking up to Spirit, in other words, realizing that there is something more to life than what we are usually told in our daily lives by the authority figures surrounding us. First of all, we all have souls, and our souls are who we really are. We are in a physical body only for a relatively short time, and during that time we have lessons to learn and all kinds of situations and locations to experience. Deep inside, at the soul level, we know this, but getting the concepts to our physical minds can be quite a challenge. I believe we choose a time to "wake up" in a Spiritual sense during our lifetime. When this comes about we may not be cognizant of it, but we suddenly notice some differences. We just feel a little looser and possibly lighter. This is one of the indicators that we are waking up to Spirit. Some of the old burdens we've been carrying ease up and can even slip away. Values change and what was so important may not seem that way now.

Waking up to Spirit is usually quite gentle, and further on in the book I'll spend a bit more time talking about the sensations. This book will try to offer you a view of what it is like to wake up and to reassure you that not only are you totally "normal" but you are also moving into the most exciting time of your life as you grow Spiritually. It is happening all around us and is growing by leaps and bounds because inside, at a deep level, we recognize our true Spiritual selves, and communication is opening. There are reasons you are related to this or that person and feel close friendships with some folks, while uncomfortable with others. There is a plan in place that you developed for this lifetime, and as you awaken you begin to open up that plan and yearn to fulfill it. This may be very subtle and confusing at first, but as they say, "the teacher you need will appear at the time needed," and if we keep our eyes open we find teachers all around us every single day. Welcome to the Awakening World of Spirit! I believe you have come along at just the right time, and you are needed!

BACKGROUND

I was born in Alabama, raised in Iowa and Nebraska, and baptized a Catholic. However, I never attended Mass until the fourth grade when my family moved to a town large enough to have a Catholic Church and school. So, from birth until about age nine my life was absent of religious "training" and dogma. I believe that time shaped the way I think and moved me in unusual directions. Was this by accident? I don't think so. A certain openness of thought and willingness to question what I saw within the church resulted in a disengagement not found in many of my Catholic schoolmates. There was beauty in the rituals and language (Latin at the time), in the May Crowning of the Blessed Virgin, and in the sacraments and music, but for me, meanings were unclear, and there were unanswered questions, which, being a small boy, I kept mostly to myself. I wondered about this God. Who was He? The Catechism class laid it all out in rather confusing, vague terms that didn't "resonate" with me so well. Though I attended Mass for the most part faithfully though my school years, I didn't feel the connection and unquestioning acceptance I was told I should feel. But, like most of us at that time, I toed the line and made it through, only to pretty much turn away from the church when I went off to college. I sensed the church could be a good place, and the many aims were positive, but the biggest issue I had was with the man up there in front. He had a direct line to God that I didn't have, and I was to accept that by faith without question? To question

2

was to sin, and sin led to forever residing in Hell. How did he get this communication with God? What made him so different from the rest of us? Was he infallible? I just didn't know and it bothered me. But there was enough beauty and mystery in the world to put this aside for the time being and move on.

A few years later, and I have no idea where it came from, I found myself in possession of an old book titled *Your Mysterious Powers of ESP* by Harold Sherman, published in 1969. Within the paperback's pages were such enticing topics as psychic powers and healing, out of body travel, telepathy, communicating with the dead, and unlocking your own intuitive sensitivity. All in all, it sounded interesting, but as I moved through the book I found it took on a very Spiritual direction and explained for the first time things I had felt since I was a child. Mr. Sherman claimed *we all had a direct line to God*, we are all part of God, we are His children, and He is a positive force. No one had more claim to Him than anyone else! Wow. My life changed from that point. I began to find other books on the subject, including Eastern religious thought and practice. Why was I not told of this before? Why did my church not include these ideas? Well, I thought I should try to find out.

Many years have passed, and during that time I have done many things, including twelve years playing rock and roll music for a living, returning to college to get a degree in education, becoming a sixth-grade schoolteacher, finishing master's and doctoral degrees in education. For fifteen years I've worked in a large metropolitan school district helping teachers utilize technology in their classrooms, a position I was very much drawn to. I also married and raised four children with my wife, Kathie. But always in the back of mind was an unsettled, restless desire to understand life for myself, to find *my* truth rather than take someone else's word for it. Mr. Sherman's book helped me realize that maybe I had not found the right information, asked the right questions, or looked in the right direction. Now the time seems right to explore, to ask, and look around. Why are we here? Where will we go when we die? What is it all about? I've found my own path and hope to share it with you. It is all about awakening to who we really are. And it is wonderful.

Why am I writing a book about this? Because I feel like I am supposed to. But what do I have to contribute that hasn't been published in book after book on the topic of Spirit? Let me put it this way: I "chose" to awaken to Spirit at this time. A wonderful psychic friend explained that we plan these things before we are born, and now was the time I was to find myself interested in Spirit; in other words, now was when I would "wake up." Sure enough, my interest—and my life—has changed a great deal. I have the same family, same wife, same home, same job, and all of that, but not the same me. As the Spiritual awakening process proceeds, new clarity of understanding presents itself. That understanding needs to be shared. What is unique about this book is the down-to-Earth approach I take in the writing and the lack of jargon that can quickly confuse newly awakened folks. There are a lot of questions you will have, indeed, that I still have, that I am not afraid to ask. I will state the questions and look for information from my higher self, my Spirit Guides, the Holy Spirit, and God.

These are weighty subjects, and the answers are important. The information in this book will either resonate with your soul or it will not, each of our paths is different, but as you read I hope you find that the Spiritual approach just feels right, and after lifelong searches we all want something that makes sense. Surprisingly, the answers are actually pretty simple and straightforward. We tend to complicate most everything in modern society and sometimes miss the forest for the trees. We can live a fulfilling, fun, happy life on Earth if we understand how Spirit works and this book will help.

IT STARTS SOMEWHERE

My entire life I've felt there was more to life than you are born, you live, you die. I believe most of us feel that, but we are at a loss when it comes to finding what the "more" to life is. What does it look like? How do we define it? Or should we just be quiet and behave? And don't ask questions! We are raised with certain religious and moral rules, which no doubt are necessary, but are sometimes ambiguous as to why. Why can't we eat meat on Friday? Why would someone be thrown into Hell for eternity for making a mistake (mortal sin)? How is it that we can be forgiven for our sins if we talk to a man (confession)? Why is it that that man, the priest, must talk to God for me, and I can't do it myself? On and on those questions went, and were not satisfactorily answered, at least not for me. So, I removed them from my day-to-day concerns and moved on. Things didn't feel right, or were misunderstood, or maybe something was missing. I didn't realize the scope of the missing information then, but the time has come to deal with it, and while working on my personal journal answers started to form. Over the years I've read a great deal and absorbed many philosophical and religious approaches to life, and in that time I've found there is a thread of information in many of the unfamiliar readings and religions that is absent from our own Catholic/Protestant churches, at least in this country. There are, of course, many sects that follow their own doctrines. I speak from my own religious upbringing, and this book does not attempt to take in every approach.

The thread I speak of, which appeared in so many places, is that of "Spirituality" as I will call it. Some of the recurring topics within Spirituality include reincarnation; karma; our personal connections with God; the reasons we are here; and where we are trying to get to. Those topics clicked with me. They felt rounded and complete, and as I studied them and allowed myself the freedom of using my gut feelings and intuition to evaluate I found them to "resonate" with me and I felt I was close to home for the first time.

This book is not in any way against established religion. There are many paths to truth, and most religions are filled with good, honest, loving people. However, in some of the chapters I will use the Catholic religion to provide contrast to my points, but this is my own journey and that may or may not resonate with you, the reader. That is OK. The issue is bigger than religion; it is the ALL of existence, the true nature of our being. This is my journey, but I'll bet you will find many similarities on your personal journey, and I sincerely hope some of the ideas in this book will help you along.

Awakening. Here is where it starts. You've been going along in your life pretty well, but deep down you feel something is missing. This feeling can move in slowly over years, but it grows. You really aren't sure what it is. Everything looks pretty good, overall. No complaints, but it seems like something is missing in your life. Not sure, but you find it comes back to you more often, sort of a nagging feeling, and you ask yourself, "Is this all there is?" Then you see something on TV, or a movie, or read an article, or possibly have a conversation with someone and your interest is piqued. Maybe it was about angels, or mediums, or a feeling you had that you couldn't explain. Your grandfather is suddenly in your thoughts for no reason at all. It is usually something you accidentally stumble into, but it seems interesting. So, you check it out a bit, and before you know it you are sort of drawn in, though with lots of questions. A medium on TV talks to the audience member's dead mother, and tears are flowing. How could the medium possibly know this? Is it a prank, a hoax, or...? You've heard about fake psychics and so on, and isn't the Internet full of that sort of stuff? Can't be believed, right? After all, this doesn't mesh with your religious upbringing, does it? Your church doesn't go for this nonsense, so it has to be a waste of time, or maybe it is just entertainment. But, those folks on that show sure do act surprised, and those tears look real. You feel a few tears yourself watching it. No, it can't be real ... but, what if ... just what if ... well, now you are really thinking. So you watch another segment and realize you sure would like to be on that show and see if this person can connect with your mother who passed on five years ago. Wow, that would be something. And you begin to wonder. Suddenly something unusual happens. A picture falls off the wall. The frame doesn't break, but as you pick it up you see the picture of your mom looking at you. There are several pictures on that wall, but this one fell (cue *Twilight Zone* theme song). Spooky? Maybe. Unusual? Yes. Message from beyond? Don't know. But what if?

OK, that was rather a dramatic scenario, and though that kind of thing happens all the time, most of us don't see the connection, the communication that is taking place. It's just a coincidence, right? Sure. Nothing more. But let's move on. You've found this interesting, and though you wish it could be real, your cool, calm, reasoning ability pooh-poohs it right out the door. But the next day you get in your car, still kind of thinking about your mother, and as you back out of the driveway a song you've not heard for a long time pops on the radio, a song she used to sing to you years ago. What? Hmmm, is this for real? And suddenly you're talking to her, "Mom, is that you? Are you trying to tell me something?" You don't hear a thing, and you begin to feel a little foolish, but wow, for a second you thought you could feel her there with you, and it was a great feeling. For a bit you didn't feel alone, and memories flood your mind. The song changes and you bring yourself back to the present, and you drive on to work. By now your attention is just a bit sharper than usual. Stepping into the elevator you say hello to the other folks, and though you are getting off on the fourth floor a rather tall lady you've not seen before gets off on the third floor, and as she steps past you there is a strong hint of Chanel No.5 perfume. Of course, it is your mother's favorite.

7

So what has happened here? Coincidences? Maybe. Or is it something greater? Is your mother simply trying to tell you that she is still with you? There are untold numbers of events like this taking place around us every single day. Most of us were brought up to believe these kinds of occurrences are nothing more than amazing coincidences. Maybe they are. But what if they are not? What if they are attempts to tell us something? That though Mom has passed over, she is OK? Maybe you have not lost her for eternity? It's an interesting concept, and for many these thoughts are the beginning of the awakening process.

The term Awakening in this book refers to becoming aware of the Spiritual side of life, the true nature of existence. Opening up to the wonders of the universe. And as we awaken we start to ask questions. First of all, is this real? And if so, how does it work? And why am I, now as an adult, just learning about it? There are many questions, and luckily, many answers. It becomes part of your "Spiritual path" on Earth to find these answers, and as you learn you become more content and feel closer to the truth. It all boils down to the simple concept of Love. Make no mistake, you love your spouse, your kids, your dog, and that is all fantastic, but this encompasses all. Love for all, and it starts with love and understanding of Spirit.

We are born with an intuitive understanding of Spirit, meaning the Spiritual nature of existence. As small children, we knew there was much more to life than meets the eye, but for most of us that knowledge was lost as we grew up—until we reawaken. Around me personally, I see this moving quickly as more folks become aware. If you are reading this book the chances are you've started wondering about life, asking questions and searching. You want answers that make sense, not so much at the ego (brain) level, but at the gut level, the heart, and the soul. Something you feel deep down that has eluded you so far. And as you awaken Spiritually something starts to come into focus.

There will still be questions, but the missing pieces are falling into place just a bit.

Waking up to Spirit can lead to many concepts including reincarnation, psychic abilities, communication with those who have passed over, understanding the reasons why we're here, Spirit Guides, angels, and our direct connection with God/Spirit. This book will not take on all of these topics in detail, but they will all be touched on.

Back to why I am interested in all of this in the first place. I've always felt (known?) that there is more to life than our basic senses show us. There has to be more to it. So, what is the missing part? Maybe all of this, but in one word: MAGIC. I don't use the word in the usual way we view it, I use it in a one-to-one connotation. In other words, one small boy who feels there is something all around him that he can sort of feel and taste, but as he ages it fades. But it can be found again; that is the magic. It would include all of the dimensional stuff: the elementals, psychic phenomenon, other worlds, astral travel, the soul. Magic. That is maybe what I'm finding again in the discoveries of this year. Talking with others and simply being still and listening (meditation) have reawakened the magic that had lain dormant for so long. I've revisited these concepts over the years, but it was not the right time, until now. If magic is not the right word, it at least works for me; it is basically outside our usual physical world and can't be seen in the normal, grounded sense. We are conditioned by life to listen to our "egos" and deny that magic. "Your mind is playing tricks on you!" "You are imagining it!" "Oh, don't be silly." Over and over we heard these things and we learned to back away and let fade our connection with the magic we knew was there. For many of us, however, the sad loss of magic can end; we can reawaken our true magical selves with all the aspects of lost memory intact! Through meditation and quiet and contemplation the magic can be found. It can become a way of life, a path to the profound, a way to reach our mysterious goals and dreams. Magic. My own term for Spirit. And boiled down, magic and Spirit are love.

I was thinking about what it is that pulls me to the metaphysical topics that I am writing about. These things do resonate with me. So, that brings me to this topic: What does "resonate" mean, exactly? Not what does it feel like, but what does it mean about the topic at hand? If it resonates with you, does that make it true? And *why* does a topic resonate with a person in the first place? These are wonderful questions that, yes, *resonate* with me. Can something that is false resonate? Can you be fooled into thinking something is resonating with you? How does vibration work with us humans? Obviously resonating equates vibration, right? So, the issues that resonate with us best are those most closely aligned with our own vibration? The lower the vibration of the individual, the lower the resonation identification? Seems to make some sense. The higher the vibration of an individual, the higher their intents become? Is this true? Is this always true? Is this sometimes true? Or are intentions unrelated to rate of personal vibration? From what I've seen, most higher-level individuals have more positive aspirations and ideals, but is this necessarily the case all the time? So much to learn.

CHAPTER 2

AWAKENING

Let's back up a bit and think about what has started each of us on our own Spiritual journey. Often termed awakening, or waking up from a narrow focus on the physical world, awakening in a Spiritual sense can have elements of joy, confusion, and even worry, but it is not usually instantaneous; rather it is a process that may take days, months, or years, and only ends at the time we leave the physical plane. Make no mistake, the Spiritual journey we are all on is the true way, the reason we are here, but how do you recognize that you are awakening? First of all, you find yourself curious, or questioning. There has to be more to life than this, right? Something doesn't feel complete. Am I missing something? These are universal human questions, and they can become quite interesting, though also often frustrating. But they are signs of waking up Spiritually. The joy comes in finding that there are countless others in the first stages of awakening, with the same feelings and thoughts. You are not alone, and you will find each other. It may start with one person, may be a discussion group, might be online, but they are there, with the same questions. You really are not alone.

OK, so you are starting to awaken in a Spiritual sense, but feel incomplete; you want answers, you want to understand. You find others in the same boat. Then what? Shared ideas from books, videos, and discussions help you focus, and an energy shift occurs. These new (at least to you) ideas are quite interesting, and you ask more questions, and you get more answers. People are very passionate about Spirit, and as you talk to them you feel "lighter." We begin to think this way, "There just may be something to this, and it just feels sort of right. But where was this information, and where were these people before? Is this some kind of secret? Yes, I've heard of reincarnation and some of these ideas, but didn't really give them a second thought. After all, this doesn't fit in with my traditional views. Is this the occult? Is it dangerous? They can really talk to my dead grandparents? I just don't know! But they really are nice, and they are excited about what they are discovering, and there seems to be a lot of information out there. And most of all, I feel sort of drawn to this. It kind of fills in the gaps and even answers many of my questions. OK, I'll give it a look and see what happens. Nothing to lose, right?"

Here's a little inside information for you. Books and discussion groups, videos, and other communication tools will only help you so far. The real change comes about when you recognize the validity of what you are reading or hearing and take it within. When the ideas become a part of your daily life, in a personal way, and becomes real individually. In other words, if you think you need to be around others to feel alive in a Spiritual sense, realize you are strong even alone! Spirit is truly within you.

WHY NOW?

Your interest is stirred, the decision to open up a little is made, it seems to make sense, so you begin to accept it as possible, leading you to the next logical question: Why am I awakening *now*? Maybe you didn't really know much about this before because the time was not right, and it is now. Without going into the details, let's just suppose your soul chose (before your birth) this time in your lifetime to awaken. But why *this* time? Maybe there were lessons you needed to learn first (in this lifetime before the current awakening) that will be valuable in the coming phase of your life. As you open to Spirit this will make sense. Look at your interest level. Is it suddenly strong, sort of came out of nowhere? A book found its way into your hand, or a movie, TV show, or a speaker started you thinking. Maybe a friend invited you to a psychic reading. It can be any number of ways, but an event really piqued your interest. This is how it often starts. And as you become more aware of the Spiritual side of life you'll open up to new ideas that often don't match the teachings you've been brought up with. This Spiritual stuff feels right, it resonates with you, but the information you are gathering does not always agree with your church's teachings. Uh oh. Now what? Keep in mind that you are not alone; there are literally millions of humans on this planet waking up right now. Some of your friends and relatives are feeling the same thing, and you will be surprised to find out who they are.

Let's review. OK, you are waking up to Spirit. You have sensed something within that is yearning, that seeks more knowledge and understanding, and you feel closer to finding answers to the big questions. You have read a few books or talked with others. Communication has begun, and it draws you in. Could you have been wrong all your life accepting what others told you? You didn't really question anything before, but now you do? When you ask questions are you running into dead ends at times? The teachers and instructors you've depended on in the past don't always have satisfying answers? As you awaken you will find new teachers. What exactly does it mean to wake up to Spirit, anyway? Well, I believe that we incarnate (are born) to learn certain lessons, true, but also to be God's way of experiencing the solid, earthly dimension. We become God's eyes, ears, etc., and what happens to us and how we respond/react are communicated to God. As you delve further into the Spiritual teachings and experiences, you begin to realize that we are truly connected with God. We are not alone, we are not islands of individual personalities floating along without an anchor. In fact, we are part of God.

The awakening part is simply a time when we have chosen to remember more of who we truly are (Spiritual beings) than we had before in this lifetime. We all come from somewhere, and that somewhere is God. We have much to learn and share while here, and we choose how it will happen. Those who have not started the awakening process can be just as kind and loving as anyone else in the process. Some lives are meant to be full of love and are naturally that way. Their soul shines through even without their knowing it. Natural. No effort needed. We all know people who are by nature wonderful, warm, caring individuals. If you engage with them in a discussion about Spirituality they may or may not know anything about it. They may or may not care. *They are living it*, and that is a choice they made before incarnating. Those of us who chose this time to awaken did so for a purpose. We had lessons to learn, some of them very difficult, some not so much, before we would realize or remember who we really are.

When a person becomes aware of their true nature, that they are Spiritual beings having a human experience rather than the other way around, they may see everything in a different light. But the great thing about awakening is suddenly so many of the mysteries of existence are closer to making sense. There may be the rush to learn as much as possible, that is quite common, and in the flush of excitement it is easy to get carried away. This is when sharing becomes vital, and energy exchanged with like-minded individuals and groups can be helpful to the expanded view of Spirit. The first excitement in discovering there are others who will validate your thoughts and feelings will lead to the second discovery—you now need to really dig in and see what it means and how it relates to you. This is living in Spirit consciously. Before you awaken, it is unconscious. Maybe you treated everyone great, were loving and kind, that was just your nature, but it becomes even more meaningful when you understand who you really are.

Waking up to Spirit is a very special time, and it changes the way you look at life. The future seems much brighter, and you find that you are better able to move forward in all phases of your life. I remember some years ago feeling that there wasn't much of life that felt positive. I thought I would just continue in a job I was not really happy with, and someday I would retire on a pension and then wither away and die. There wasn't much to look forward to; in fact, it seemed pretty grim. I was happily married and my children were all doing well. I was content with my life overall, but it felt like something was always just out of my grasp. I had not begun the awakening process so I couldn't see the big picture. Now I see my life in a much different way, and I hope there is sufficient time to do everything I feel I am supposed to do! I have ambition and drive, and best of all, I have a destination, or a direction to go. That was lacking before I woke up. In this book I will explain the changes I felt and how it changed everything.

ENERGY

One of the simplest and yet most powerful concepts in the cosmos is the concept of energy. Vibration. The stuff that makes it all happen. Everything is made of vibration or energy. Let's look at how it affects us. A couple of basic ideas need to be restated: first, energy attracts energy, but mostly similar kinds of energy. In other words, positive (faster) energy attracts the same kind of positive energy, and if everything is made up of energy, including our thoughts, words, and deeds, then we would be wise to think, talk, and act in positive ways. If the focus is on negative (slower) energy, we draw in more of the same. This is why someone who seems to have nothing but bad breaks is that way. Positive attitudes bring more positive energy to us. Again, you know some who seem to have nothing but good luck and all the breaks. Energy can work for you. Prayers, good thoughts, best wishes for someone are real, and each channel positive energy to the person you are thinking of. Even more amazing, there is an abundance of energy available for your use; it is unending, no limit at all. God's energy is flowing around and through you all the time. One image I read about somewhere that has stuck with me is that energy (could also be called love) flows like a waterfall. Never stops. It is flowing right down at you, and all you need to do is picture yourself stepping into that "waterfall" and feel it coming into you. I see it entering the back of my head and filling me with Spirit. This is yours for the asking. We all have full access, and those who learn to use it lift their lives up tremendously.

Picking Up Steam

So awakening to Spirit is something that is happening all around us and seems to be picking up steam in recent years. This is what I've experienced myself as I've discovered friends, relatives, coworkers, and neighbors who are at this same point. The Internet is full of videos and online groups who are interested. Facebook has many Spiritual accounts set up where you can find friends. Communication is much more advanced now than even a few years ago, and validation of Spiritually minded people is much easier. The yearning for more meaning and a sense of who we truly are is strong throughout the world. There are those who are far advanced in the process and have been on their path for some time. These are Spiritual guides and they are all around us. Look and you will find them.

A leader that helps you is invaluable, but be aware always that they cannot walk your journey for you. Only you can do that. You can learn and study and discuss as you awaken, but the true value is within and to move forward you will have to quiet the mind and allow your soul to communicate with you. Meditation, music, walking, exercising, anything that takes your mind away from the constant worry and unending words will allow your higher self, which is your soul, to communicate with you. You may hear words; you may get feelings, see images, or simply notice a calmness, but you will get results if you truly calm down your active egoic mind. Most of the ideas for this book have come directly from my quiet times, which allow ideas to form.

As we grow older and realize that our time on this planet, in this life, is getting shorter it is natural to look for ways to reduce the fear and uncertainty of our last days. Our background in this society and within our established religions may not have prepared us very well, or at least it doesn't seem quite right. Many older folks are beginning to look at a Spiritual approach and are waking up now, but not only older ones. Every age is represented in this movement, but there are a tremendous number of children who are born awake or who wake up very early. They may not have the words to describe much of what they know, but they do know. They will see through and reject so much of our past. Religions will have a difficult time in the future holding on to these children. You may have heard some of the terms: indigo, rainbow, or crystal children. These are special Spiritual beings coming into this world to help lift the vibrational speed of the entire planet, they will help lead the next generation to Spirit. They are here now and more are coming. If you are a young person yourself, and are reading this book, you probably are one. Welcome! If you are not so young and are awakening now, like myself, welcome to you, as well. Keep in mind that labels and names are not important; it is the moving forward to Spirit that counts and working as a team: children, adults, older folks, all races, nationalities, and backgrounds will see a change in the world in our lifetimes. Every one of us is a pure Spirit of God clothed in our human forms, and at the soul level we are all one with God. No one is better than another; no one is less than another. Beware of labels and so-called levels of awareness and psychic ability and so on; those things are very much temporary. We are all headed in the same direction, and our journey involves working together in support of one another to keep on our Spiritual path. It truly is a new world just waiting for more to wake up and join in. It is a worldview based on love. Pure love.

Flow

When we are truly on our Spiritual path we seem to flow, to move easily. Life comes to us without so much stress and anxiety. We become like water and flow downhill, skirting around objects in our way. That is an interesting image. Let it go, and just flow with the path you have set for yourself. Stop resisting. Wow, what a thought. Stop resisting. Don't struggle, don't fight it, don't try to manipulate, don't control, let it roll. Don't think about it so much, just flow. Flow. Flow. Flow. Right down the hill of life, along the water path, simple. Gravity moves us, and our path moves the same way. If we run into obstructions, we will stop or slow down. But if we truly flow, we will continue around or over or under, and best of all, no effort is needed! Life becomes easy. This is our goal in this lifetime, to find our true selves, our true paths, and to flow with them. The effect on ourselves and on everyone around us can be dramatic. Life becomes simple and fun! Much like it was when we were children, before the worries and fears of life entered in. Finding Spirit puts us where we need to be.

I realize this sounds too easy, or as if it must be a trick. It is not. Let me explain. Yes, you will still have to do your work. You will have many challenges to work through, but your attitude will determine how much of a problem these challenges become. If you are truly flowing in Spirit the issues will be bumps in the road, but quickly dealt with and you will move on. There are big problems that arise at times, family crises, financial worries, and so on, but learning to ask for guidance and help will assist you on the way. You have Spiritual advisors who will help, but you must ask them; they cannot interfere or assist you without your permission. Flowing with Spirit teaches you how to let go of the past, of painful memories. There is no reason to allow the past to haunt you now. Today is a fresh start; today is brand new! Let it go, and when you are in Spirit you live in the present moment. The past is truly gone. You don't need to forget it, or pretend it didn't happen, but you no longer dwell on it. Your life is now.

CHAPTER 3

SPIRIT BACKGROUND:

WHAT, WHERE, WHEN, AND WHY?

If you find a lot of this new, and confusing, well, you are normal! As you awaken you go through a great deal of bewilderment, and part of your Spiritual Path is to untangle that bewilderment, find where your path leads you, and then follow it. Sounds easy, right? And in a way it is, depending on the "baggage" you are carrying and how you chose to deal with it. But how do you know you are on the right path? You feel it; you experience a lack of tension, an ease that wasn't there before. It feels right. How do you know when you are not on the path? Everyone slips off now and again. You will feel anxiety, fear, and worry. Look at your life. What brings you effortless joy? What brings you fear? Begin to really look at these things and give yourself permission to move away from one and toward the other. Ask yourself whom you are trying to please. If it is others over yourself, you are missing the mark. Look for what brings you happiness. You are in charge of you, first and foremost. If you are happy and content others will feel it too. Of course, bringing true happiness to others is a wonderful way to bring happiness to yourself as well.

But how did this all start? I didn't answer the questions of why we are here or who we really are. There are plenty of experts out there who can give you their side of things, and here is mine in a nutshell. We have existed for all time and will continue to exist forever. Wow, mind blowing right off the bat, eh? Yep. You can look at this in two ways: the "prove it to me with Science" approach or the "feel it in your gut" Spiritual approach. Spirit is about your soul, not your physical body, not the Earth, not this dimension we live in. I use

20

the word Spirit to represent the over-all encompassing power of love that we often call God. Is God real? Yes. Is God universal? Yes. When I talk of Spirit I am talking of God. Is this the God of the religious training that we were often brought up with? Yes and no. God is everywhere and is described in many ways, but some religions distort our relationship with God. The biggest blunder in many of the established churches is teaching that God is separate from us; that God is an angry, spiteful, punishing God. No, God is all love; man for various reasons created the angry part.

CHURCH AND RELIGION

Some words for Spiritual fulfillment include Presence, Awakening, Enlightenment, and many more, but all refer to the same thing, and as we awaken we can begin to feel this. Is it difficult to verbalize and make understandable? Is this only for the Yogis and other adepts? I don't think so. It can be simplified, and I believe it should be. We have to go with a higher self or soul-level understanding, somewhat outside our usual thinking process (ego) and more attuned to Spirit. That is where this is understood, and developing an awareness of soul leads to a new way of thinking and relating. It involves trust, faith (which is huge, NOT the faith we are called upon in our churches to believe "because we say so"); this is inner faith, which we create, nurture, and rely upon individually. This faith comes from our own intuitive knowing and heart/soul-level feeling. It may feel new in this lifetime. We have been taught and led in a different way, and we did not question it. Think back to our church-based childhoods. We were told what to think, how things worked, what to believe, and how to act, but were not encouraged to really think, question, or ask for explanations. We were to follow suit and behave as we were told. I think this has been a big deal in my life. Let me explain. As I mentioned in the introduction, I was raised away from the church from birth until about nine years of age. I had no church or formal religious indoctrination, so I was free of the concepts. Yes, my siblings and I knew right from wrong, and so on, but no idea of God and sin, Heaven and Hell. We attended a nonreligious public school. My family moved the summer before my fourth-grade year to a larger town with a Catholic Church and school. It was as if we moved to a foreign land. I had missed the religious training from the earlier years that my classmates had gone through. I had not been socialized in the same way, and I was sort of an independent thinker, but I didn't know anything, so I went along. I learned what they were teaching and really enjoyed some of the rituals. As I mentioned in the introduction, there was nothing as amazing to me as the May Crowning of the Virgin Mary statue out between the old church and the nuns' home. I loved the pageantry and wearing the cassocks and surplices. It was truly magical, but as I grew older even though I might go to church on Sunday I did not feel the deep connection that I sensed should be there. I should feel drawn to it, that it was real and correct. But when I attended a Christmas eve midnight Mass and saw some of the so-called leading figures of our church reeking of alcohol, there because they had to be, not because they wanted to be, the inconsistency hit me. The religion felt phony. I lost my belief at that point—not in God, but in the man-made church. It wasn't just that instance; this feeling had been building for some time. Too much of what I saw did not fit the teaching. "Do as I say, not as I do" didn't work any longer for me, and it was time to search for other avenues of understanding. I began reading Eastern philosophy and religious texts, but I felt alone. No one to talk to and work with, but I continued finding more books. By the way, this is a sign as well, books will show up; you may see them in a bookstore, in the library, at a friend's house, but somehow they end up in your hand. Not every one of them will be just right for you, but many can help you grow.

When I met my wife I realized she was deeply entrenched in the Catholic ways, and I went along. I still enjoyed some of the rituals, but something was still missing. Truth and meaning should be within each of us, not handed down by others. We are on our own journeys. Now, I find a great deal of support for these concepts, and it has awakened that side of me that was dormant for so long. The time had come to awaken to Spirit.

REINCARNATION

Some basic information is needed at this time about reincarnation. Without a bit of understanding some other concepts won't be as easy to accept. Reincarnation is a popular topic these days and much is being heard about it on television, in the movies, in books, and so on. Reincarnation is basically the idea that we return from the Spiritual world to Earth more than once. Can be many, many times. So why would we do this? To begin to understand who we really are; to experience the physical dimension, and to grow. I like to believe that if we "happened" once why can't we happen again? Western religions mostly teach that we are here one time and that is that. Reward or punishment. Heaven or Hell. End of story. Just doesn't make sense or feel right. Many Eastern religions take reincarnation as a given.

Haven't you wondered why we are born, live a life, and then go to eternal rest? What is the purpose? A lifetime flies by and there are so many unanswered questions. For example: we are taught that we will be placed in either Heaven or Hell for our behavior while on Earth. What if we've never been told that? Is it fair if I've been born in some place remote that has not been exposed to religious doctrine, and never heard the concepts of right and wrong and sin? Will I still be sent to either of those places if I am not aware? I cannot conceive of a God that would be so unfair. When I was in my early twenties two young men in white shirts and dark ties came to my house and wanted to talk about saving my soul. I allowed them in, and we chatted for a while. They said we had only one life and had to be baptized to enter Heaven when we die. They also claimed that only so many individuals would be allowed in. Everyone else will suffer an eternal punishment. Well, of course I had the same questions as I mentioned before: What about the native uninformed peoples somewhere on an island out in the ocean or in an undiscovered jungle who are not exposed to religion and are not baptized? Will they go to Hell? Yes, they told me, those people were not saved. I threw them out. No God would do such a thing. I began to see that some religious thinking was off track, and as I was introduced to more concepts and ideas I saw that reincarnation made sense to me. I have often wondered why a place felt familiar when I had never been there before (in this lifetime, anyway). Why certain movies or books drew me in. Why did I read so many books about wooden sailing ships? I grew up in the middle of the country, in Nebraska, nowhere near the coasts, yet there I was, reading *Mutiny on the Bounty, Sea Wolf, Moby Dick*, and so many more while still a young boy. Why the deep interest? Visiting New England for the first time recently, it felt so familiar, yet I had never been there (in this life, anyway). Reincarnation just feels right in my gut. It makes sense to me that we've been here many times with lessons to learn, and we will continue until we reach a certain point that we no longer need to return.

But why wouldn't we want to return? Most likely the Earth's physical plane is the lowest level we will ever experience. In fact, some say that Hell is right here. There is pain, poverty, war, anger, and much more that don't seem to be of Heaven. These move us away from Spirit, yet often need to be experienced to allow us to grow. We don't face the difficulties of this life from the next dimension. So why do we come back again and again? We come back to learn in this form (physical) and to share with God. We are God's eyes on Earth. We are part of God. But we also have free will, and that is where we sometimes get into trouble. We start to believe we are separate from God (we never are) and that we are isolated individuals. Our actions don't hurt anyone else, right? Wrong. We are all equal Spiritual beings, all part of a loving God or Spirit, and what we decide to do with our free will affects everyone else. The process of awakening we are experiencing is the opening up of our mind to our soul, and we consciously begin to understand our true place in the universe. We are not alone, we are not separate, and we are one.

The phrase "trying to get back home" has been popping up lately in my studies, work, and writing. This chapter is all about our journey, and the ultimate destination is to get back home, or Heaven. I write a great deal of music and just wrote a song about this. Here are the lyrics:

I'd Go Home

[Verse 1]

Here I'm standing, Lord how I wish that I was gone

I know it's underhanded, but I feel like moving on

If I could find my way out of here I could stand it

If I could just find my way out of here I could stand it

If I could just find my way ... I'd go home

[Verse 2]

If I can slow down, maybe I can catch a break

But I speed up, I'm so afraid that I will be too late

If I could just find the door

If I could find the secret door
If I could just find the damn door ... I'd go home

[Bridge]
Sometimes I feel there is no reason for me to stay
I've been here enough and no longer want to play
But I still can't find a way ...

[Verse 3]
Time goes by me, but I feel like I'm standing still
It reminds me, that my heart lies behind that veil
If I could just take the first step
If I could just take the very first step
If I could step out the door ... I'd go home

[Verse 4]
My friends wait for me, I can feel them guiding me
along
Can't be too late for me, they let me know when I
am wrong
Someday they'll take my hand, I can feel it
Someday they'll take my hand, I can feel it
Someday they'll take my hand ... and I'll go home

What is Heaven, though? We've all been there, but most of us have no conscious memory of what it is like. We read about it, talk about it, and imagine it as the ideal, wonderful place where we will remain for eternity. It can be that, I suppose, but it can also be whatever we picture it to be. I truly believe it is more complicated than Earth, than Heaven *or* Hell. There are multiple dimensions along the way, and the next level, often called Heaven, is simply a step above the physical level. There are many levels above that, all getting closer to the true Spirit of God, and as we grow and learn we continue to go back home where we started. The point is that when we leave this level we will find a much happier, more beautiful existence without pain, without the limitations of this lowest of levels. The change is significant, but we don't just disappear. We are still who we are, and we know those who left the Earth before we did. We remember those who are still Earth bound. Sometimes a person will be so strongly attached to their earthly life and family that they have a difficult time moving on. They may need to learn to let go, and it can take a short time or stretch out for a while. On this side we must try to be understanding when we feel someone still hanging around, though this can be sort of scary. Did someone say ghosts?

This leads to mediums and psychics. Who are they? What do they do? Where do they come from? First of all, yes, there are true mediums that can communicate with the entities that have passed on. There are also phony mediums who use deceitful ways of pretending they have these abilities, usually for monetary gain. There are even those who combine both, ability with the desire to make money. Nothing wrong with that, but intent is a powerful thing. It is perfectly all right to make a living with the talents we have; but to be dishonest, or to use the abilities for anything but the greater good of the client would not be a good thing. How do mediums talk to the dead? I've asked several that very question, and they actually communicate in many ways, some hear words in their head (usually in their own voices); others picture images that they interpret; and some actually see the departed and mentally talk to them. It is not an exact science, and each medium has a unique way to go about it.

Psychics are very similar in that they are able to know information that would not be readily available in the physical world. That information comes by way of communication through the next dimension as well. I don't seem to use these abilities myself much except for allowing the free flow of ideas to enter my writing from my own Spirit Guides.

But here is the clincher: we all have these talents. Yes, I said it. We all have them. We are all psychic and have mediumistic abilities. So you say, "Then why can't I do those things? I would like to talk to my grandmother who is gone now!" And that is where it gets interesting. These are skills, much like being a painter or a singer, or any one of dozens of other abilities that we may have. There are excellent painters and average painters. There are good singers and not-so-good singers. There is natural talent in everyone, but often in different areas. At a young age I was drawn to the guitar, and I can play various styles and have recorded a few albums of original music. My two brothers were not interested in this and have other abilities. It is the same with the esoteric talents. One person can be very strongly psychic with uncanny results when conducting a reading; they tap into the universal truth most of us can't sense. It is a talent. Can we develop this? Yes, like anything it can be improved with practice.

Why are we born with different levels of ability then? What is the reason for this? This question is a big one and is at the heart of our differences on Earth. I believe that before we are born we map out our coming lifetime. We decide on certain goals or lessons we wish to take on and then work out what would help us grow Spiritually the best way possible. This may mean we purposely leave out certain talents and abilities as we design our plan or that we are very strong in other areas. Remember earlier in the book where I mentioned that there is no such thing as coincidences? It is the same for natural skills and talents. We have them, or don't seem to have them, for specific reasons. If a person finds they have strong medium talents it is hoped they will chose to use those talents in positive, beneficial ways to help others move forward on their Spiritual journey. Just to complicate things a bit more, it is also possible that we live many years with no noticeable knowledge or interest in Spirit and then suddenly we wake up! I've talked to several people who saw John Edward doing readings for a group of people on his TV program, *Crossing Over with John Edward*. This show changed their lives, and something sort of buried inside came out and led to tremendous discovery. There are certainly many, many other triggers that have started people on their paths. This is just one of them.

Those folks who are blessed with psychic abilities are often confused, especially when they are young and told by unknowing adults that what they are seeing and hearing is their imagination. Not real. So they stuff it down and try to ignore it all. This sometimes works, and sometimes does not, and when validation comes through by seeing a program like that mentioned in the last paragraph it can make all the difference. They are not so strange, not merely imagining everything. They might actually be normal, and this might be a gift!

The key is to accept who we are, what talents we have or do not have, and to realize we chose the situation we are in and with lessons to learn we need to make the most of it. Keeping an open, positive mind will allow our true path to unfold before us and give meaning to what we do. As souls, which are our true selves, we have all the skills, talents, and blessing that God has provided, but as humans we are more limited, and as I said, for a reason. Acceptance of who and what we are will take us down the correct path.

Chapter 4

Recognizing Who You Really Are

With all of this talk of Spirit and reincarnation and so on, we have to ask ourselves, "Just who are we? How did we come to be here on Earth? Why are we here? What are these so-called Spiritual gifts that psychics seem to have, and do I have them, too?" These are big questions and small ones. They feel enormous to the newly awakening individual, but less imposing after a while. Most of us were brought up in traditional kinds of ways, including religious beliefs, family interactions, and accepted societal rules. Many of those traditional approaches are egoic in nature. In other words, they were instigated by man and not necessarily connected to Spirit. As I had mentioned earlier in the book, I didn't understand how the man at the altar in church had a direct link to God that I didn't have. Well, now I see that "big" question wasn't so big after all. The egoic nature of many churches teaches us that the man at the altar is a representative of God and through him we communicate with our Father in Heaven. This does a couple of things: (1) It places a great deal of power in that man's hands if we must depend upon him to forgive our sins, explain to us what God wants us to do, etc., and (2) though we are told to pray to God, it is not really explained how we can develop a personal one-to-one relationship with God, that is, without the middle man. The nature of many religions keeps the power in the hands of human entities, along with the decisions on what is right, what is wrong, how to do this and that; that is, man-made rules. Certainly nothing wrong with following them if you feel the desire, but to try to enforce something just because you say so? It can become all about control and can very well backfire in the long run because it will often lead to questioning the egoic rules and power structure. It happened that way for me, and once you start questioning and don't find satisfying answers you turn away and begin to open up to other, more personal beliefs.

WHY ARE WE HERE?

First of all, we are all sparks of God or Spirit; each and every one on Earth, and throughout the universe. The lowest person you run into on the social or financial scale is an *equal spark of God.* The richest most powerful person is an equal spark of God. We are all equal, and we are all aiming for the same thing, to be reunited with Spirit. Due to ego, many do not realize it at the incarnated human level. A rich man may want more and more. The reason is probably because he is not satisfied. The satisfaction he desires he cannot put into words, but it is a soul-level need he cannot fill with more money and possessions. The ego is never satisfied. On the opposite side of the coin is the poor man who is content. Yes, some do exist, those who live in Spirit. Living in Spirit means a reduction in ego's influence.

We all have special gifts; in fact, we all share the same ones. But those gifts appear to be stronger in some than in others. Why is that? In the last chapter I discussed reincarnation, and if we accept that as possible we can then examine why we are "gifted" with certain talents while on Earth. Let's say that we all have the innate ability to be psychic, to be mediums, to communicate with those who have passed on. Then where are they? In the world of psychic phenomenon, I am a flop, at least as far as I can tell at this point. OK, let's revisit reincarnation and the lessons we want to learn while on Earth. I believe that before we are born (each time) we actually prepare a plan for our life. In that plan or outline certain things will happen at certain times to enable us to learn the lessons we have chosen. We give ourselves the opportunities to learn whatever it is we need. For instance, maybe we need to learn patience, so we find ourselves marrying someone who really struggles to be ready on time or in a job where a coworker fails to get tasks done when due. We have to deal with that, and in this time around maybe we learn to be patient. Anger, yelling, cajoling, whining, and threatening do not help, and it comes to us eventually that being patient and dropping the stress of expectation calms us down. It may take a while to learn this, but hopefully in this lifetime we do learn a valuable lesson. We can only control how we react and how we feel, not how our spouse or coworker respond. That is their path.

There are many psychic gifts and talents, including empathy; some individuals who have an ability to *feel* the emotions of those around them. This can be a problem for empaths, who are somewhat like TV antennas and pick up the often-confusing energies of others. Empaths can be overwhelmed if they don't know how to protect themselves. This can be very difficult, especially in an emotional, excited, or angry crowd. So many highly charged feelings and thoughts are flying around, and the empaths pick them up, often draining themselves of energy. Most of us are empathic to a certain extent, and you can see it in yourself if you are often confided in, if others come to you for comfort or help. They sense you understand their situation. But be aware that often empaths are taken advantage of. Less positive individuals will also sense the empath's vulnerability and openness, and they will actually try (unknowingly) to drain their energy.

If you've been around someone for a while and feel overwhelmed and exhausted every time they leave, you've been with an energy "vampire" and it is best to protect yourself. There are several ways to do this. One way is simply to avoid the person. If that isn't possible, then you have to shield yourself. This can be done by picturing yourself as a strong Spiritual being with mirrors or a clear, impenetrable bubble around you, and all the negative "junk" tossed your way simple bounces off, leaving your energy right there with you. After a while you learn how to protect yourself at this level, and you will see the person have less and less to do with you. They won't even know why most likely; yet they no longer can steal your energy and use it for themselves. These kinds of people do not like to share their own energy; they just want everyone else's. Anybody who seems negative all the time, who complains about unimportant things, who just can't seem to get a break, well they are in this group, and unless you feed them energy they will move along. They don't realize they are drawing in more of the same slower, negative energy, which expands the bad feelings they have. They are creating their own mess, so to speak, though it is *always someone else's fault*. This is a vicious cycle, and you do no one any good by adding to it. Move away.

WHAT TRIPS US UP? MIGHT NOT BE WHAT YOU EXPECT!

It is a good idea to be aware of the things that trip us up. What sets us off and gets us upset? Those very things may be on our list of lessons to learn this time around. We can overcome anything if we want to. For instance, you have difficulty remaining calm driving home in rush-hour traffic each day from work. Your temper trigger is very thin. After all, you worked all day, feel tired, and just want to get home. Why are these people driving so slow (fast, stupidly, recklessly ... choose your word)? And then there are the traffic lights! Always red and you never get a break. Oh, and don't even get you started on the street construction! Wow, how do they know exactly which lane I'll be driving in so that is the side of the street they tear up, with never anyone actually working on it? And so it goes. If it's not one thing, it's another, and all are working against you. Hard not to take it personally after awhile, eh? Well, depends on how you choose to look at it. You always get to choose! The roles are *victim* or *learner*. The victim role is pretty well spelled out above: anger, frustration, and woe is me. The learner role allows you to look honestly at what is happening. There is *always something to gain* from all of this. Maybe your lesson for today (and as long as you don't learn it?) might be to find patience in your heart and learn to deal with the drive with a different attitude. The attitude you choose makes all the difference. Breathe deeply, let the angst go, and as you sit in traffic look around a bit. There are things happening everywhere and lessons to learn. There is beauty in the trees and flowers along the way; beauty that you've not noticed before? If you breathe and slow down a bit you might just find out there is a world out there that deserves your attention. Find some music that is soothing to listen to. Adopt a new attitude and you will find things change. Remember the old saying "*if* such and such just happens, I'll have a better attitude!" Well, the truth is, "*if* I have a better attitude, such and such will happen!" That's the way it works.

Now let's think a minute about the people we meet in life, even those we see every day, and who we are related to, work with, and so on. You get along pretty well with *most* of them; you really enjoy and like *some* of them; and you feel sort of neutral about *some* of them too. But what about the ones you just don't get along with? Those whom you really don't like? What is going on there? There may be several things happening. First of all, have certain events occurred in the past to make you feel this way, so your dislike is event based? Or is it observing and then judging their behavior that has caused your feelings? Or is it possible nothing has happened, yet you still don't care for them? Maybe you disliked them the minute you met? This does happen, though we usually overlook it for the time being just to get along. Here's what I think: first of all, if we agree that we are Spiritual beings in human form, here to experience life and to learn, then we can suppose that there is a great deal of communication going on at other levels besides our human level. The dislike that makes no sense may well be from that level. Possibly it can be traced to earlier incarnations in which we had bad relationships with the same person. It has been suggested that we often incarnate with the same group of souls. OK, so what do we do? This is the important part. We must teach ourselves to look at the other person and change our view. Instead of disliking someone, let that go, and think of him or her as a Spiritual being who is here to teach us something. They are offering us learning opportunities, as we are for them. Release the dislike and look at the lesson! You don't have to try to like them, but you do need to learn. Maybe the learning is about patience or how to keep your cool when starting to feel angry. It may be a "mirror" lesson to show you a way you behave at times. See it, accept it, and allow it to absorb into your soul. Lessons can change your outlook on everything! Please understand that this approach does not mean that you have to stay around those that you don't feel a liking for or that you have to pretend friendship with them. Oh no, you can safely move away. Being aware that they may be offering a lesson is all you need. Stay open to what you can learn, but there is no need to put energy into the relationship.

Every Single Person Is Spiritual!

One of the most important concepts for us all to learn is that every single person in the world is a Spiritual being, no matter their social status, no matter their income, where they live, if they are healthy, homeless, disfigured, or even comatose. They are true Spiritual beings connected with God exactly the same as everyone else, including you and me. There may be physical and social differences in our lives on Earth, but look deeper to the real substance of life and find the eternal soul we all share. When we realize this, not in words, but in meaning, and accept it in our hearts it begins to manifest in our daily, human lives. You are driving along the street and see a homeless person, and instead of thinking badly of him you realize that this is a person just like yourself, but in a different learning environment. They may be offering you a lesson at that moment. How will you respond? Free will allows for choice. Maybe there is something you can do or maybe not. Awareness may be what he is offering you, and if you see who he really is the lesson is learned!

A simple way to look at our mission here on Earth would be to see that we drop in (incarnate) many times, and though a lifetime to us here seems long, it is actually not in the overall view of things. We drop in, go through a lifetime with many others, move on back, and repeat. Each time we learn more and more, and we move forward on our path, learning who we are and where we are headed. Suddenly the so-called big issues of our daily lives seem less daunting, less imposing, and maybe a little easier to deal with. We begin to reduce our hectic lives to a simpler, less-cluttered approach as we realize that our problems are not usually all that big and can be solved simply by going right at them. Of course, these are *our own problems*, never someone else's. They have their own path. Keep in mind we are all God's children, all here to learn, and all of us will return to Spirit. Everything here is very temporary; that's why riches, power, and fame are so fleeting—they don't go with us! Only love stays alive with us. The more love and caring we share with the world, the better off the world is, and the same goes for us.

As we awaken to Spirit we see everything in a new focus. So much of what seemed important simply isn't. The annoyances of our day drop aside, just not worth our energy and attention. We rise above those things. Sure, situations still come up that force you to deal with them, but we begin to realize that so much of what we have been worked up about has been of our own creation. We are allowing and even encouraging these fearful thoughts and worry. I keep coming back to watching the news and how it is slanted to keep us worked up. Haven't you noticed that the biggest sponsors of news are pharmaceutical companies? This is not by accident. The news gets you all worked up and worried, but the pills advertised will fix you up! You see commercials about new diseases and health problems almost every day during the news, and luckily they've found a pill to help cure whatever it is you suddenly feel like you might have (oh, never mind the long legal list of problems and side effects you may encounter from taking the cure!).

And so it goes. Fear and worry rule the world of the egoic person. Only by becoming aware of what is happening through awakening can you stand above it. First you must see clearly, and then you can make the right decisions about your short time on Earth in this incarnation.

SOME OF OUR SPIRITUAL ABILITIES

As I've said, we all have talents, abilities, and gifts, whatever you want to call them in the Spiritual sense. So let's examine some of those you may not have been aware of. First of all, let me ask you this: Have you ever felt sad or down around someone that is having a rough time of it? Maybe you've simply been around them and felt some of the pain they are going through. Taking this a step further, have you been around someone you don't even know yet feel strong negative (or positive) feelings for seemingly no reason? How about being in a crowded room or in a group of people, or at a sporting event with thousands of people? Do you feel overwhelmed? When you get back to your own safe environment, do you feel fatigued? Drained? As I wrote earlier, my friend, you have *empathic* abilities. We all do, but trust me, some have them well developed. They feel the pain of others (not so much physical, but rather emotional) and instinctively know what the person needs. Nurses are usually very strong empaths, as are teachers. Empaths are good with people because they understand what the others are feeling. This is a Spiritual talent or gift! Learning to work with it is important or you can easily be overcome by loss of your own energy because empaths often give their energy to others without knowing it. Again, awareness is the first step. Empaths must learn to protect themselves and use this talent in the most positive ways they can. Empaths can use this to understand those around them, yet learn how to guard their own energy. If you or someone you know does not feel comfortable in a crowd, don't try to force them. Picking up so much from too many people can overwhelm them. Later, as they learn to control it, they can venture out as desired. As I said, we are all empathic to some extent, but those we want to talk to about our problems and we are drawn to are probably gifted in this area.

Another often-overlooked Spiritual ability is that of intuition. We've all had hunches about various things in our lifetime. Some of them were right, some were off, but we still felt those, didn't we? This is a common ability that is ignored, but it is real. Learning to develop your intuition is often an excellent way to help you understand Spirit. This book isn't about how to develop these talents, but in a nutshell, intuition is working all the time, and as you learn to listen to it you will find that more and more of your day-to-day decisions are positive. Which way to drive to work today? When you learn to trust your intuition you'll choose one way and on the radio you find out there was a water-main break or road construction on the other route! You may have been slowed down causing you to be late for an important meeting if you chose to drive the other way. Intuition is active all the time; you just have to learn to recognize it and listen. This ability is available to everyone who wants to use it.

What does intuition feel like? Well, you mostly will have a feeling, like I said, a hunch. It is the first choice that is usually right. Once you stop to think about things in detail you might lose the intuitive information. You easily talk yourself away from it. At first you may not read your feelings quite correctly, but with practice it becomes second nature. Trust in yourself and it will grow.

There are other talents or abilities that are more pronounced in some including mediumship, which is the ability to communicate in some fashion, be it hearing, feeling, sight, or sensing images, with discarnate Spirits, those who are not of the physical Earth at this time. Everyone is somewhat psychic, but not everyone is a medium. Mediums can provide communication with our departed loved ones.

Remember, we all have some abilities, but these abilities are more developed in some, so don't get frustrated if you don't feel their calling. These talents can be developed if desired, but are not necessary to lead a fulfilling, happy life of Spirit.

CHAPTER 5

SIGNS: COINCIDENCES?

Communication and signs from the departed are mostly subtle. That's often a hard lesson to learn. I will admit I've always hoped to see angels appearing or to hear spectral voices. That seems to happen a lot in books, right? So, I've been somewhat disappointed in that area. However, when it was suggested by a psychic friend that I keep a journal I thought I would give it a try. Once into the flow of writing daily it became easier and easier, and suddenly I realized more was going on than I had originally thought. The (usually) daily entries were getting longer, more detailed, and new, expanded topics were coming up I hadn't previously thought much about. In fact, it seemed to others who read some of the journal that I was being "given" information from another source in some manner. At first I didn't think this was possible; after all, the words form in my own mind as I'm typing, so I was doing the creative part, right? As I continued writing the entries became more detailed and flowed with little forethought from me. Information, suggestions, and explanations that I had never thought of were suddenly there! Weird, but magical, too. I learned to trust the words that came through me and let them go. Upon rereading them I was often surprised and still am. The writing validates so much of what I've felt and learned over the years, but this is the first time I found direct communication from elsewhere. No angels appeared, no voices rang out, but ideas came to me! As I learned to roll with it and even enjoy the process I felt nothing but calmness and peace. It is not difficult; I just seem to know what words to type next as I go along. Magic.

This chapter is about signs and coincidences. The biggest sign I've gotten is from my journal, but signs and connections come in many ways. Earlier in the book I offered a scenario of a woman beginning to awaken to Spirit, in which a picture of her mother fell from the wall, she heard a favorite song on the radio that her mother liked to sing, and even that she smelled Mom's favorite perfume in an elevator, all in a short space of time. Are these anything more than coincidences? Those who have not begun the Spiritual awakening will probably say they are meaningless, just foibles in the day, accidental happenings with no meaning, or possibly wishful thinking. Maybe, but what if there is more to it? What if these are direct signs? As always, the key is awareness. An important word in waking up is *awareness*. I've come back to this several times in this book. Becoming aware of the outer happenings in our dimension is what waking up is all about. Little things that happen that remind us of a departed relative or friend, hearing a song that offers an answer to a problem, or hundreds of other things each day that could be full of meaning are suddenly noticed. Before, we showed them right out the door. Now we slow down and wonder. With awareness we can see so much more. A phone call comes from an aunt that you've not heard from for a while, and you were just wondering how she was. These things happen quite often, but we often don't see the connection.

There are several ways to help you notice these not-so-coincidental "coincidences." One is to keep a journal of seemingly unimportant incidents that cause you to have an unusual feeling, whether it is happy, sad, an "ah-ha" moment, or just something that catches you by surprise. Often the meaning isn't clear until later. This is why keeping a journal is helpful. It is easy to forget what has happened after the fact or to blow it off as of no value. When you are writing in a journal, especially if you keep it actively with you, and jot down whatever occurs, you become much more attuned to the messages from your Spirit Guides, passed loved ones, your Guardian Angel, and more. They are communicating with you all the time, and often they have a wonderful sense of humor. If you see something that strikes you as funny while going through your day, there may be a message there. Don't look too hard, though. If it is meant as a message, it will be fairly easy to see, or it will make sense later. Don't try to force a meaning on everything that happens to you; trying too hard to find a Spiritual meaning for an incident can lead to frustration. Better to let it go and allow the meaning to come to you when you are ready. Stay open to it. When you raise your vibrational pattern, more of these messages will come through. Don't be afraid to talk to your Spirit Guides and loved ones to ask them for signs and to help you with decisions. They will help you. Your path is ahead of you, and there are many bumps and turns to be dealt with. Having your guides right there to work with you, showing you subtle signs on which way to go can be invaluable. Sometimes the signs will just be a hunch you feel. But awareness must come first. Understanding and then incorporating this information can lead to a feeling of togetherness, that you are not alone. There is, after all, a team around you at all times. But they cannot help unless you ask for it. They will not interfere and will do no harm to anyone. Your guides are all positive, based on love for you and Spirit, and they want to help you move in a natural way, at a natural pace in that direction.

Guides may change as you grow, but your Guardian Angel is with you the entire time. Talk to your angel, ask for validation, and ask to feel your angel's presence and love. Talk to Spirit. Ask the Universal Consciousness (God, Spirit, whatever name you wish to use) to be with you and help you along the way. Ask.

Here are some other fun, interesting, and sometimes amazing ways to help create clearer contact with Spirit: turn on the radio at a random time and see what is playing. What memories does the song bring up? What images? Or open a book to a random page and place your finger down. Read what you see. You might be surprised at the message just for you at that spot.

After a while these things start to become the "normal" way for you. You pick up a magazine and find a how-to article that is aligned right with something you were trying to figure out.

Yes, there are many "coincidences" each day that you can begin to notice, and the messages get clearer as you become aware of them.

ENERGY, AGAIN

When you boil it all down, everything is made of energy. The universe is made of vibrating energy. We are too. The chairs we sit on, yep, energy. Vibrating at different frequencies, thoughts, desires, words, actions, all are real and all are made up of energy. *Thoughts continue to exist after we "think" them.* Positive or higher vibrating thoughts will attract positive energy back to you. If you believe things are going to go well, they usually will. I didn't say they always will; there are sometimes lessons that can only be learned by something painful happening, but you will experience Spiritual growth through the process. By keeping your mind on the lesson and positive results you will get through it. Conversely, focusing on the negative side of anything will attract more negative energy to you, the opposite of what you wish for. As they say, "like attracts like," and you can see it everywhere around you. For instance, on the playground at recess, a group of children will often put themselves into groups with those they feel most comfortable with, those that are most like them. This is sometimes called the Law of Attraction, which is "like attracts like," as mentioned above. Energy works the same way, so the more positive energy around you, the more positive energy you will attract. We all know someone who seems unhappy and down in the dumps all the time. Everything they say seems to be tempered with complaining and feeling the world treats them unfairly. It's always someone else's fault, never theirs. They don't realize that they are extending energy that actually causes more of the bad things to happen. They are attracting more negative energy that results in their own unhappiness. As we awaken, this becomes clear. If you refuse to go in that direction with them, eventually they will either raise their vibrational rate to balance with you, or you will move away from each other. This happens all the time, and it make take days, weeks, or longer. When two people have mismatched frequencies, they will not feel the urge to be around each other. Much like magnets turned one way or the other: attracting or repelling, a vicious cycle that can only be broken by changing the way we look at things and by raising our vibrational rate. Positive, successful people do not focus much on the negative side of life; they believe things will go well, and they usually do. Of course, you always have the option of dropping to the lower level and trash talking the boss, the weather, indeed, the world! But this serves no good purpose for anyone.

If you are asking for signs from beyond, remember they can be quite subtle, but being aware and putting your positive energy into them makes them stronger and easier to notice. For some this comes very quickly, for others it may take some practice. The first step is to open up to it. Don't dismiss everything that happens as a coincidence. There is much more order to the world around you than you can imagine. Stay open minded, let things come as they will, and ask for signs. One more thing: it is also possible that signs will hit you in the head! Some won't be subtle at all. Keep your eyes open; they really do want to communicate with you! For fun, be aware of license plates and billboards as you drive. You just never know what you may see!

DON'T JUDGE TOO QUICKLY!

One of the dangers of awakening to Spirit is the egoic tendency to be judgmental at first. We see things more clearly; we see behind some of the veil; we understand a little better why some people act the way they do. Don't judge! Don't fall into this trap. We can examine our own reasons, but it is not fair to judge anyone else, even if we think we know why they are the way they are. We can react, we can stay positive, but we should *never* judge. Some actions may appear to be negative to you, but there are many wonderful people playing various roles on this planet. They may have lessons to learn for themselves, but did you know that they may well be volunteering at the soul level to help you with lessons *you need*? For example, you are walking downtown and a ragged bum asks for spare change. Don't judge him too quickly! Many times we will turn away and move along and make comments like, "Get a job!" or some such aimed at him. Let's take a second look at the bum. First of all, what if he is truly needy with no skills, some medical problems that won't allow him to work, and mental illness? This may well be his only means of livelihood. Now, a closer look yet reveals that, no matter his clothes, his looks, his demeanor, he is one of us, a spark of God, of Spirit. The same is true for each of us, and we are no better or worse in God's eyes than a priest, pastor, doctor, lawyer, or any other person. He is beloved of Spirit. He is as we are, a soul having a physical experience. His higher self, or soul, is communicating with yours. Even if you don't consciously feel the communication, it is happening. How do you respond to this person? He is your brother. The Bible says, "Judge and ye shall be judged." As we gain Spiritual awareness we realize what we are doing, and we back off from our first judgmental thoughts about this man or anyone else we meet. In an egoic world, everything is compared and evaluated, and it takes a true shift in consciousness to move away from judgment. At first, this feels unusual, but seeing what we do from outside ourselves can be very enlightening. With practice this awareness will grow and become part of who we are.

Awareness leads to the most powerful and valuable lessons on Earth. Imagine if the world could do away with all judgment! If we saw one another as simply extensions of ourselves, as part of the world of God, of Source, trying to get back to Heaven, or the next dimension. We can do this alone, or we can work with others. How we wish to move forward is up to each of us. But it cannot be in words only; it has to be internalized and become an implicit part of our lives, of our personalities, where we no longer have to stop, to catch ourselves, in order to do what is right. We simply relax and make the Spiritual choices and know those choices are right. We will feel it in our gut, which is a strong indicator that we are on our path. Believe me, we will know. And best of all, when making the right choice we feel great, and it gets easier as time goes along. We are drawn to more of the positive energy that we manifest by doing the right thing, by recognizing the true Spiritual identity of all those around us. It's life changing and freeing at the same time.

This chapter is about coincidences and signs. If we go back to the idea of the bum on the street panhandling, think a moment. Everything that happens is for a reason, and that man may be providing a learning opportunity that you specifically asked for and planned in this lifetime. How do you respond? I'm not saying you have to do anything; that is up to you, but just be aware that there is often more to a situation than meets the eye. So why did I bring up this particular situation? Well, it happened to me twice just recently. In all my years I've pretty much turned the other way to avoid panhandlers. Yes, I wondered if they were lazy and just needed to clean up and work like other honest folks do. I thought they might be taking advantage of the generosity, or guilt, of those they bump into. Well, here's my own story. Both times I was driving and at one busy corner I happened to see a fellow with a sign asking for help, anything. I had never done this, but something compelled me to grab my wallet, pull out some money, and pull over a bit so he could reach my hand. I looked in his eyes and he gratefully took the $10 like it was a hundred, and said, "Thank you so much!

God bless you!" We communicated for maybe five seconds, but as I drove away I felt terrible. You didn't expect that, did you? I felt terrible that I had ignored so many pleas for help in the past. Such small things can make a difference. A few days later, many blocks away I was pulling onto a freeway exit ramp and at the end, just before you turn was another man with a small sign asking for help. I had to do it. I pulled the dollars I had out and not only moved over a bit to reach him, but stopped traffic behind me. Again, so grateful, "God bless you!" and off I went. It dawned on me that the few dollars I spent might go anywhere, I don't know where, and it is up to the men I gave them to. I hope they were helpful. But the real value in my mind is that there were other drivers behind and next to me who witnessed the small gesture I made. They either thought I was a soft touch for bums, or I felt guilty for some reason, or they were actually moved by the small handout. Maybe, just maybe they thought for a moment and possibly they will react just a little more openly to those in need. That kind of action can spread. Show someone a kindness, and those who witness it may expand on it. Positive energy multiplies! When more and more people awaken we can hope that kindness continues to grow. Will I give money to others who ask for it? Who knows? But if a person on the street has the essence of Jesus or the Buddha and are offering us an opportunity to step out beyond ourselves shouldn't we take it? Shouldn't we treat every person we meet as though they were Jesus or the Buddha? Yes we should, because they all are. We all carry the true essence of God within and how we respond is all a part of our journey on the Spiritual path.

Coincidences? Maybe, but with awareness we can start to see what is behind them, that there is often a lesson to be learned, a message to be received, a thought being transferred. It may be only to say, "Hi, I'm here!" from a passed loved one. They want us to know they are alive and well on the other side. Communication occurs all the time, and as humans we are not always ready for the messages. We've been brought up in a society and culture that waves away these kinds of beliefs, and we are expected to deal with cold hard facts. We've moved away from Spiritual understandings and have lost our way. By understanding that the unusual sights, sounds, smells, and coincidences may well be more than they seem can help open the door and can change our lives. It is happening to me and so many around me.

I've heard many times that there is no such thing as coincidences. I don't know for sure, but I suspect that is so. Each event in our lives, no matter how insignificant it may seem to us at the time, is valuable, has a lesson of some kind for us. When we are in the Spiritual flow, we learn to handle those unexpected events and coincidences with an open mind and open heart, and we draw in positive energy to help deal with them.

CHAPTER 6

WHY ARE WE DRAWN TO CERTAIN THINGS?

In an earlier chapter I discussed energy, so let's take a more in-depth look at it now. Scientific words like frequency and vibration are often used to describe why we are drawn to certain things and people and not so much to others. Why does this movie affect me strongly while my friend just doesn't feel it? A book is very moving and my wife loves it, but when I read it, I don't get it. On and on this goes, so many personal likes and dislikes, comforts and discomforts. You might say anything that feels positive to you "resonates" *with* you, and you would be correct. That is a good way of thinking about it. Let's say that everything has its own frequency, it vibrates at a certain speed, including our own bodies and souls. The higher the frequency, the closer to God we are. This is why we hear the phrase "raise your vibrations" so often in Spiritual reading. The ultimate goal is to raise our frequency to the level of God, to become one with God. But we aren't there yet; at least most of us are not.

But why are we drawn to certain people, places, things, and so on? Sometimes it makes no logical sense. For example, there are many kinds of music, so why does one person love classical music while another will only listen to country music or rap, or rock, or Frank Sinatra? As I said in the last paragraph, everything has its own vibration or frequency, and those that are most like ours will make us feel better. Can we change our vibrational frequency? Yes, more on that in a bit. So, is it science, then? Yes and no. The scientific approach may explain it on the physical plane, but we are so much more than that. On the next level, the Spiritual plane, we are connected, too. Our souls vibrate at a certain speed, and we want to raise that rate, so it is an all-around desire to resonate at higher levels. These are the levels of joy and love, of happiness and acceptance. The lower resonating levels are the ego's areas of expertise: fear, anger, unhappiness, frustration, and feeling out of control. Lift your level and you will lift your heart and Spirit, and your higher vibrations affect everyone around you! It is contagious, and they may not even realize it. They feel better. We actually affect everything around us, including the entire world and universe! Imagine if everyone was on the same high wavelength! That is what we are striving for, of course.

But let's be realistic here for a moment. Yes, we can have an effect on the universe, but maybe we should start with ourselves. After all, that is the only control we actually have. Just what can we do to raise our own level? So many things can help, even very small ones like smiling at someone, being kind and thoughtful, being thankful for anything and everything, being of service, helping someone. It is easy to get things started, and raising your vibrational level affects everything around you in small subtle ways. Colors may be a little more vivid, music sounds clearer, people respond to you better, and best of all the more positive interactions with others the more your vibrations gain strength. Your frequency calls similar frequencies to you. It all comes back to "like attracts like." Let's get back to you as an individual and how you can raise your level. Other ways include simply wishing only the best for others, refusing to badmouth someone, refusing to partake in rumors or gossip, staying away from bad behavior, thinking kindly of others, even those you don't care for much. These are the daily, simple techniques, and they are pretty obvious, but did you realize that your thoughts affect you and those around you? Thoughts are real, and because they are energy fields that stay around you, they work like magnets and draw more of the same kind of energy to you. The more positive thoughts you have, the more positive energy you pull to yourself, and the more those around you will react positively in return. Energy reacts to the energy nearby, and you can actually control that within yourself.

SIMPLE STEPS TO RAISE YOUR VIBRATIONS

Begin by simply refusing to gossip. Always realize there are other sides to every story and it is not our place to judge someone else. They are on a completely separate path and journey, and we simply cannot know what their challenges are. Since we can't know, we cannot judge. We have only our own life to judge, and even that is wrong. We must love ourselves and forgive ourselves and continue to strive to improve. As long as we remember that we are part of God, that we are Spiritual beings living in the flesh for a short time, and that we are connected to God at all times, then we will be gentle with ourselves. As we become more aware of the true Spiritual nature of who we are certain things become clearer. An example for myself would be how the nightly television news sounds completely different. This will be clearer in chapter 8, which deals with our egos. Let's just say that the ego loves drama, fear, and worry, and is a part of us. Our Spiritual side is the opposite; it loves peace, harmony, beauty, and happiness. So what does the news have to do with it? I used to watch the news, though I've never felt I really needed to, but as I've awakened I see another side of it. The way it is written, the way the reporters talk, the leadoff stories of the day, are usually negative, full of worry, fear, and what might happen! It seems so clear to me now that the news is egoic in nature and depends on the people watching to feel fear and be upset and worried. That is the nature of the news, and it has gotten much worse in the last decade or so. You can certainly see the same approach in the political advertisements on the radio and TV just before major elections in this country. Not much in the way of helpful ideas, are there? Mostly attacks on the opposition, even looking back at a misplaced word or stumble from years before will be blown up out of proportion and used against them. The nastier the better, and almost all of it seems to be taken out of context. It is not a pretty game they play, but they get results. The negative (slower) energy of the ads draw in more from those watching, and even more important, those watching pull the negative energy to themselves from watching the attacks and negative campaign comments. The watcher who already believes the worse about a candidate (may be due to their stance on something, or their political party) will quickly agree with the negative approach and fuel it, creating a big, ugly circle of combined vibration. But as we become aware that this is happening we can move away, or ignore, or look for more positive ways to get information. I must admit that I almost feel physically sick when the news or ads of this sort come on, and the overall approach of TV has led me to watch less and less. If you can't avoid watching, or at least being in the room when these things show, try to lift your own vibrations above the negativity. You can focus on something positive or simply refuse to pay much attention.

MEDITATION AND QUIETING THE MIND

You hear that meditation is the key, and it is very helpful. It isn't the only way to lift your level, but does help with change and making it more permanent. Quieting the mind from the nonstop chatter in your head can also be accomplished by working in the yard, folding laundry, driving, or cooking. Really, anything that slows down the noise is very useful. Being around positive people, and conversely, staying away from negative people is important. As you awaken to Spirit you will find that some old friendships are no longer desirable. This will happen on a subconscious level. Someone you often got together with calls you up, and for the first time you find you don't really want to go along. This is not a bad thing; this is simply growing in

Spirit. It is not an all-or-nothing condition, however. You can still get together when you wish, but you will find you have different feelings about it. This person no longer resonates with you. You've become more conscious of your own vibrations, and if theirs is slower you will have less interest. This can be good for both of you. The other person can then choose to raise their consciousness to enjoy your company, or they can stay where they are and watch you part ways. This is totally natural, and again, neither of you may realize what is happening since it is going on at an unconscious level. This kind of interaction is happening all the time for everyone around us. You will find that you want to be around other people who have a higher rate of vibration and who are more in tune with you as you grow. Keeping yourself at a lower level than your heart and soul yearn for will not make you very happy. So be aware of this. Do not be judgmental, however. Remember, every person is on his or her own path, and yours may take you away from some former friends, which is perfectly fine. Don't look at them with anything but love in your heart. You are not better if your vibrational rate is higher; it is simply where you are on your path. Each person is a perfect Spiritual part of God, and no one is left out. It is always possible to change your own vibrational speed, but it is not your task to change someone else's. Everyone finds answers in their own way and in their own time. Watch that you don't drop down to less positive levels when around certain friends and family. It is very easy to do, but you won't feel good about it in the long run.

It is just possible that a person you know who seems to be causing problems for another has actually volunteered to do just that to help the other person grow! This is why we should never judge and why we have no right to disapprove of another person's behavior. We can remove ourselves from the area if it doesn't feel right to us. There is no shame in moving away. The old egoic attitude of "stay and fight!" is simply wrong. There is absolutely nothing to be gained by violence or verbal attacks. They simply escalate into unmanageable affairs that lower the vibrations of everyone around. Of course the ego loves it. The lower the rate, the stronger the ego is. This works for those nearby, too. An observer to a fight who cheers on one of the fighters is hurting himself and everyone else involved. The mob mentality often steps in and the egos of several people are working in unison, sharing energy and allowing a feeling of righteousness and anger to consume all. But some are aware enough that they will feel inside, at a deeper level, that this is not right. They will know, but may not be strong enough to take on ego and leave. They don't want to be seen as uncool or afraid, so they stay to save face. This is pure ego at work. Later they may feel the result of that decision. They may even develop some physical symptoms. Maybe their conscious is bothering them a bit. These are all higher signs that the soul wants you to move forward and away from the slower vibrations.

The challenge comes down to a question of who is drawing us toward a person or a situation or location. If the ego is in charge, we are probably attracted for reasons that are not so healthy to our Spiritual being. If Spirit draws us, it will vibrate at a higher rate and lift us up. When we develop our awareness, we recognize this difference and start to shift toward positive, uplifting energy. As mentioned earlier, some friends will drop away while new ones will show up. There is a shift in our views, and a clarification of why certain people are around us. We can see more clearly and make better decisions with Spirit on our side.

These energy vibrations exist in people, as I've said, but they are also present in the workplace and in all physical locations we visit. Some places you visit make you feel better than others. Some towns feel more like home, and some feel darker, less friendly. This is vibration, not better or worse, simply vibration. The ones who most nearly match you, or are above you, will draw you in. I will never forget the first time my wife,

Kathie, and I landed in the airport on the island of Kauai, one of the Hawaiian Islands. We stepped off the plane, smelled the air, and felt something we had never felt before, a vibrational rate that sang to our souls, and we've gone back many times since then. Yes, it is beautiful there, and the weather is usually quite pleasant, but we both agreed there was something more to it, a feeling of being home in a sense. Everyone has stories like this, where a place was just right, it seemed familiar, so comfortable and friendly.

AT WORK

How about your job location or the occupation itself? How do you feel when at work or doing what you do? Is the environment negative, neutral, or full of positive energy? You can overcome some of it, but wouldn't it be wonderful if you could always feel the good side of the energy spectrum? Many people feel they are stuck in jobs that drain their energy, and they are right. Sometimes that is necessary; you need that job, it pays well, or well enough, and after all, you have responsibilities, right? So what can you do if it doesn't offer you the positive feelings you crave in your heart? You can try to adjust your feelings, look at the positive side of what you gain by being there. You can refuse to spend lunchtime complaining with coworkers about the boss or the hours or whatever seems to be a problem. If you recall that like attracts like, you can see it gives energy to the very things you are unhappy about! You are actually undercutting your own chance at happiness. And since egos feed upon the unhappiness of other egos, you and your coworkers are hurting yourselves. This doesn't mean that you should be outwardly unhappy and go to the boss and try to change things this way, though it might be necessary, who knows? It means that you can rise above it. Don't talk the problems to death; do something about them! Even the simple act of checking the want ads for another position can help, if you see that nothing is going to change at the workplace. You really have only one thing you can change and that is your own attitude. Look for ways to take action, not talk. Ego loves talk; ego doesn't want these things solved, so you must stand up for yourself and find a way out or around the situation. Raise your vibrations and you'll attract more positive results. Better jobs, better coworkers, and even higher salary are all available if you take the right steps.

CHAPTER 7

DESIRE TO SHARE WITH OTHERS: VALIDATION

As you awaken to the possibilities of an expanded and certainly more fulfilling life, you will naturally wish to share this information with others. You will look for those who are like-minded, and you will find them. Though the true path is within yourself, sharing what you are feeling and going through is very helpful. There are many at this same point finding their own Spiritual paths, but as self-contained entities we oftentimes focus upon ourselves without realizing the effect we have on others. Discussing and sharing helps break down those self-created walls, brings us more into the light, and strengthens our Spiritual awareness.

We've become aware there is more to life, more than meets the eye, and it has been right in front of us. We have the urge to say, "I knew it!" because we did know in our unexpressed thoughts, in our deepest feelings, in our soul. There has to be more, and there is. Doors have been flung back and everything has changed.

Can the journey you find yourself on be traveled solo? Yes. Will it be fulfilling? Maybe, but we are a social people; we interact and react according to social mores and rules. We are used to working with others, so is this Spiritual path different? Yes and no. It can be traveled alone, but there is much to be gained by working with others, by sharing your experiences, your thoughts, your feelings, and your new knowledge. Others will do the same, and what I've found in this journey is that many, many of us are on a similar path, and overall our concepts agree. For some of us this is the first time we've found agreement of this sort. And here is the kicker: I've come to the conclusion that not sharing what you are learning and feeling may be sabotaging your own path. Let me explain. Some will be content to work through the journey by themselves, and if that is their true calling that is fine. But many will have a chosen task to fulfill planned before they incarnated. It may be to become a leader or mentor for others as they awaken. There may be a need for you to share with others what you have learned on your path. In other words, the picture may be bigger than just you. Only you can know this, but trust your instincts. Your higher self and your guides will let you know at the gut level, in your heart, not your mind. Feel it. That is how this book came to be written. I felt I had to do something. I felt I had to share thoughts from my journal. And you may feel something similar. You may just have the perfect experience or story to share that someone else desperately needs! You have so much to share. Don't bottle yourself up. Reach out. There are hands waiting for you.

FINDING VALIDATION

As more people/souls have chosen to awaken at this time there is a need for validation, and as I said, this is often accomplished best through interaction with others. Having conversations with individuals and finding that there are many more opening up to Spiritual awareness than you probably expected is a starting point. Your next-door neighbor whom you've known for years may be very much attuned to Spirit. But it isn't always brought up. I've found this to be true many times recently. Spirituality and the search for meaning is universal, but not often at the forefront of social interactions. This is changing. Those who begin to awaken often tell me that it just feels right. There is something reassuring and natural in the concept. It seems to be what has been missing, and it is good. Spiritual discussion groups are springing up all over the place. Meeting regularly, they take on many of the questions we all have, and by sharing we find that we're not alone. Look for these groups; most are totally free.

The discussions often start out with a topic of interest that gets the ball rolling and soon many join in, and it is surprising how much we have in common and but haven't discussed with others before. It is very cathartic and freeing and, as I said, validating.

Another way to learn more about this new world is by reading books on the subject. There are many besides the one in your hand. Literally hundreds of esoteric/Spiritual books are flooding the market with wonderful content in so many of them. Follow your instincts and your Spirit Guides when choosing what you want to read; you'll get the right ones. I've purchased many books, and in some cases started reading one and twenty pages in set it aside. Either it simply did not resonate with me, or I wasn't ready for it, or there just wasn't anything new or interesting. Have no regrets; put it down and look for something else. You are the judge of what works best for you.

A great deal of content is also available online, on YouTube, and other Internet locations. If you are more of a visual learner, you may wish to take a look at some of them. Of course, like most of us you will probably look at a variety of sources: books, videos, magazines, and so on. How do you wade through it all? Again, use your own inner guide. You'll know. You'll find the right books and videos that connect with your soul. Your guides will lead you at the right pace, and the information you need will show up in one form or another. Have faith and keep your senses open. One way I do this is to be aware when someone recommends a book or website. I can feel if they are coming from a Spiritual place with their suggestion, and I will almost always take them up on it and get the book, watch the video, movie, join the group in Facebook, or whatever they suggest. Again, if it doesn't work for you, put the book aside, turn off the video, and move on. Keeping an open mind and heart will lead you to just the right information. Forcing yourself through information that doesn't feel quite right for you or that you are not ready for will not help. Put it aside, and if you feel the urge in the future you can come back to it. Or not.

When you begin to awaken you may not trust what you are sensing. You've been brought up to believe other things that don't match up with the Spiritual world you are starting to feel. This can be a real challenge, and in some cases you pull back and don't wish to move in this direction. If you've read this far you probably are not in that group. That is OK. When you are ready you will know, and the time will be right. There is no hurry, and like I said previously, there's no need to force anything. Opening to a world of Spirit is effortless; it provides its own energy and momentum, when you are ready, and if not, not a problem. Maybe later. But if you are feeling that you are headed in the right direction you'll have doubts, "How do I know this is real? How do I react? Why should I?" will all pop into your head. You want proof, someone to show you that this is real. We've all been there, and it doesn't stop. The most advanced, Spiritually, will still have doubts and their own set of issues to deal with. We are human; we are generally at a rather low level of Spiritual awareness, so we have to go through various growth steps to awaken, and after a time a growing acceptance is felt with less need for questioning. I don't mean in the way a charismatic leader demands less questioning of his/her power. This is really different because it comes from within. No one else is telling us how to think or what to believe; we are finding it ourselves, and this is very different from the ways we've been taught.

Keep in mind that Spiritual paths are unique to each of us. Our timing and steppingstones along the way are placed just for us. There is no right or wrong, only what we know within. One person may become aware of Spirit and their spouse may not. This is not good or bad; it just is. Don't try to push your ideas on another; it won't work. They are on their own journey, and you should accept that with gratitude and wonder.

The Newly Awakened Can Get a Bit Overexcited

In our desire to share what we are learning we can become a bit zealous, shall we say, overcharged with excitement. This may be something we've felt inside for years, but didn't have the words for it. Now it is right here and we feel it! So, off we go to convert everyone on what we now "know." Careful, this can have the opposite effect on what you are wishing for. What now seems obvious to you is still a foreign concept to many of those around you, so be careful how pushy you are. Be gentle. Keep in mind that each and every person is on his or her own, select path back to Spirit. You cannot judge where they are on that path. Like-minded individuals will find each other and move forward offering support, and others will simply not be at the same level. Acceptance of all levels is the right approach. There is no judgment; there is no better or worse; we simply are what we are. You'll find yourself moving away from some folks and toward others; this is the path of life.

Some who are newly awakening want more, more, more, and will look for books, videos, television shows, and so on to help them understand better what they are feeling. This is normal, but after a while it is just possible that the onslaught of information is not helping. You begin to see that many of the books you are reading, for example, say basically the same thing. Not a lot of new information, and you start to put them aside a bit, maybe coming back to them later, maybe not. Eventually you begin to understand the true journey is within, not in books, videos, and so on. Within. Your higher self, or soul, knows what you need to learn, and when you learn to tune in to your soul you will find the exact information you need. You will be guided gently to the right teacher, book, movie, conversation, or whatever you need at that time. A teacher will appear. Just maybe it is the book in your hand that helps you awaken. Creating it has certainly helped me put my thoughts and feelings into words.

Opening to Spirit is not difficult. It is quite simple, and as humans we tend to overcomplicate everything. It's been described as simply remembering who we really are and where we come from. Awakening is like breathing; simple natural breathing in, breathing out. We have so many blocks put in front of us, trying to make the path more difficult than it actually is. Blocks put there by our own egos, which I go into in more detail in another chapter. We tend to think that anything of value *must* be difficult. It simply *can't* be easy! Don't we have to fast and atone for our sins, and walk on hot coals or something to reach Spiritual enlightenment? No. Well, maybe for some that was their chosen path, but for most of us, no, it is simpler. It is in realizing we are Spiritual beings here for a short time. We are unlimited; we are based on love; and we are perfect.

The words you are reading are symbols, words, print on paper, computer screen, or digital reader, and they are powerless unless we accept them and add them to who we are. This is why the scientific approach alone will be frustrating. Our souls operate at a higher level, and being closely in touch with them brings about the gut feelings and intuitive thoughts that lead us unerringly on the right path. We have to learn to recognize them, however. In an earlier chapter I mentioned that we are often told that the unusual Spiritual happenings around us may not be just coincidences, and we need to see them for what they really are. This is not difficult. The difficult part is in moving away from what we've been taught and raised with. Dropping those views and replacing them with new ones is the way to move forward. This cannot be forced; it is accepted within each of us, individually, not in a group, not even with another person. This is like being born or dying. We are truly by ourselves, and no one is going with us in a sense.

If we are blessed and find the true spark of Spirit within and accept it our lives will change. Maybe not in big ways, but certainly the way we view everything will change. There will be vividness of color, aliveness in the air, an understanding of others we missed before. Spirit affects everything, and all for the better. Spirit puts us closer to our goal of being one with God and moves us in the right direction.

One of the frustrations of waking up to Spirit is hearing story after story of others who are having visions or talking to dead people (mediums) or knowing something in the future (psychics). Yet, maybe you can't say you've had any of these, and that is OK. Those are outward manifestations of Spirit that you can develop over time. Most of us do not bring these talents forward in our lifetimes. If you are around those who can do these amazing things, be encouraged! You may not be there yet, but they are providing you some views of the Spiritual world. Learn what you can, and you will know what you should do. Yes, it can be frustrating at times if you have a friend that does psychic readings and you can't see or hear anything much. But that is simply where you are on your path; if you don't have that particular ability you probably don't need it. We are all prepared and equipped for our time on Earth, with every talent we need. Trust in yourself and your own inner soul. Everything is there and ready for you.

So, you've gotten all caught up in the new excitement of the Spiritual fellowship you've discovered. Others who love to talk about and study and share have welcomed you. And you expect miracles, but they don't seem to be happening. Let me give you an inside secret. Accept yourself just as you are! Do not waste energy and time on wanting what anyone else has. Coveting is all too human. You are perfect, Spiritually, just as you are. Move forward trusting that you are traveling at the perfect pace to learn and develop. And you will! You are here with a set of talents and skills, and lessons to learn, and all will be balanced in your lifetime, so move forward with all positive feelings and anticipations, you'll find out it all works out.

Chapter 8

Allow Yourself to Let Go!

I've only touched on a very important but basic concept that is central to the human experience: Ego vs. Spirit. Or maybe more accurately stated: Ego *and* Spirit. We live in a world of duality, and we are buffeted constantly by the needs and wants of life, by the fears and worries and anxieties we feel each day. Why do these things happen? Do we need them? Is there a reason we get so worked up about this or that? What can we do? What *should* we do? As always, the first step to understanding is awareness. Awareness of ego and how it works can help explain a great deal. What is ego? In this context I am not referring to ego as the "all about me!" attitude we sometimes see. Not the big Hollywood-type egos that are paraded on TV and in the movies. The ego I wish to discuss is more basic; it is a cornerstone of who we are. It is neither good nor bad (some of you will disagree), but ego is certainly a useful tool as we grow up. Without ego to keep us in line we could cause ourselves a great deal of harm. The ego warns us that we could get hurt jumping off a roof or eating too much candy, but we often do it anyway. When we are young we need the ego to keep us safe. However, when we get to be adults and have formed our own moral code to live by things change a bit. It is time for the ego to gently fade into the background and allow our higher selves, or Spirit selves to take the lead. This is where it gets tricky.

Ego Enters the Equation

Let's define ego and how it is connected to our Spiritual life. In simplest terms the ego is the part of us that thinks our thoughts. As I said, it is necessary as we grow up to keep us safe. The ego actively looks for danger and spots problems, and this is where the trouble comes. The ego wants to exist and wants to be strong. It is at odds with our Spiritual side, or our soul. The ego exists by keeping us worried, off balance, thinking in negative terms, and overly concerned about what may or may not happen. The ego is very strong in our culture and it is not easy to move past it. It thrives on pain and misinformation and confusion and worry. In our world (and many others), ego rules. Ego is rampant, makes the decisions, and influences everything much more than we realize. The need to have the upper hand, to be seen (in our own minds) to be superior in some way is a constant activity we take part in, and don't even realize it. If we can get past the ego we will be in Spirit. But this is a tough roadblock. Being *aware* of the ego's actions is the first and strongest step toward reducing its control of our lives. Note with interest the feeling of worry or anger or whatever and release it! The ego wants you to play with those feelings and internalize them and make them powerful and controlling. They actually feed the insatiable ego and make it stronger and more powerful. To note, almost as an observer, what the ego is doing in a situation is to disarm it. Observe it "at work" and step away. This can become second nature after a while. It may never go away completely, and will rise up whenever a chance comes along, but again, note it and put it away. It will eventually give up. Open hearts in all situations will help keep the ego at bay. Go into every situation with an open mind and feeling that only the best will happen. This is simple manifestation! Believe in good things and they will come to you. Believe in worry and the "ooms" (doom and gloom) and you will manifest them as well. You are what you think! Yes, I did say that the ego is our thinking mind, but to allow the ego full reign and control is the worst choice possible, though there is a great deal of that in the world today. Taming the ego by moving toward positive thoughts diminishes the egoic desire for drama and negative energy. Manifest and trust. Trust in God, in our Spirit Guides and Guardian Angels, and in our higher self. In fact, the higher self is the key. We must get to know who we really are, where we are from, and then we can be confident in where we are going, or more importantly, where we are in the present moment, and that this moment is perfect, it is where we are supposed to be, doing what we are supposed to do, and being true to our soul nature.

Ego exists within our own consciousness, and its hold on us can be total, or in the highly Spiritual person, rather tenuous. Most of us are somewhere in the middle. Let's look at a better explanation of ego for those who are ruled by it. Let's say that something trifling has gone wrong: the new quilt you ordered for the spare bedroom has arrived and they sent the wrong color. How big a deal is this? Depends. If ruled by ego it can be a big one. Anger, frustration, yelling, cursing. Certainly this can be an inconvenience, but just how big a deal is it? You box up the quilt, give them a call, and explain it. The quilt goes back, and you are sent another one. Another example can be seen in commercials on TV. During the news they seem to be focused on aches, pains, this new terrible condition (which you've never heard of) or that one, and on and on. So much worry. The signs for these conditions are pretty broad sometimes and it is very easy to think, "I might have that ... whatever the disease was. I better go get some of that advertised medication from my doctor." This is selling by fear, egoic fear. Ego doesn't want to fade away and allow Spirit to come in. Ego wants to remain in control and in charge. Fear, nervousness, and anger are all signs of ego in action. Blowing small events into big problems is ego's way of maintaining its health and vitality. The more ego has control, the less sense of satisfaction in your life. In fact, ego actively seeks problems, and really likes to look at the behavior of others. We are so easily offended these days, and we have strong opinions about other people. Could be our neighbors, or townspeople, or even an entire country or ethnic group. Ego would really like us to dislike everyone! This feeds it and keeps it alive. All prejudice is egoic, as well as generalities about a culture, a people, a group, or an individual. Anything that divides or creates an "us against them" is the result of ego being alive and well.

So what happened to ego? Earlier I said that it keeps us safe as children, and that is true. It certainly doesn't want our bodies to die because it would disappear! A strong, healthy ego keeps the individual worked up, angry, nervous, and out of balance as much as possible. The more drama the better! "Everyone is against me!" "I don't like them, they are different!" "They are unfair!" Focus is always on the perceived thoughts and actions of others, not of oneself. THEY are at fault, always! Ego LOVES this.

When we are young we have not developed the common sense yet to determine what is safe or not safe, so the ego steps in and helps out, as always, for its own good. The ego is not necessarily evil; it just wants to exist and be strong. It is the other side of Spirituality, which wants to exist and be strong, too. Ego would lead us astray, and you can see it clearly in every newspaper and newscast on the television or radio. Ego loves to work with other egos as well. If a person gets upset about an injustice (real or imagined) and complains to others, they just might join in, building more egoic anger and energy. Mobs are formed this way, as are riots and fights; all of these are egoic in nature. When ego takes over, common sense often goes out the window.

Living a life that bypasses ego and resides in Spirit sees life in a completely different way. Difficulties are simply opportunities to learn. Bad things happen to everyone. Being able to see the real issue is key. The wrong color of a quilt is of little real importance. Yes, it means you have to reorder and causes a few minutes of inconvenience, but really, that is all. Do what has to be done, and forget it! Move on. Using the power of Spirit in your life lets you see it this way. When a problem occurs, you can either act on it or complain and allow ego to move in. And *the more you complain and give energy to ego, the more it wants.* Suddenly you are complaining to anyone who will listen. Ego feeds ego. Others get involved and it is a big bitchfest! Yep, egos are running the show. Though this is a very common state in the world these days, there is hope. More people are awakening to Spirit every day, and ego and Spirit can't run the show together. They can bounce back and forth a bit, but not as a team, more as combatants vying for control. But Spirit is gentle, patient, forgiving, and understanding. When you live in Spirit and get into a situation where those around you are complaining about this or that (The government is taxing us too much! Or I didn't get my fries at the burger drive-through!) you will understand more clearly that these are simply egoic arguments, and you won't feel the need to add to them. That is important; *you no longer add energy to the situation!* You either change the subject, or you try to move away. There is no need to argue one way or the other. Everyone is on his or her own path with their own opinions, and you have no need to change them, no need at all. True Spirit stays positive and forgiving.

Ego is devious, sneaky, and part of our journey on Earth is to learn to live in Spirit, to move away from ego's constant push for worry and fear. Remember, God made all, and everything is perfect, including each of us, so why do we allow so much worry and fear? Those are ego's tools to keep us in its grasp. Move away and feel Spirit in your life. Everything feels different when you are not putting energy into your negative fears and worries. Push those aside. Yes, there are times when difficulties have to be dealt with. So, deal with them and move on! Don't dwell; don't continue to fret and worry. If there is nothing you can do about something at this moment then set it aside. This moment is all you have. Don't let ego rob you of your true nature. Live fully in Spirit at this and every moment.

How to Deal with Ego

Here is a lesson that is hard to learn for some: if someone is having a tough time with a spouse, boyfriend, girlfriend, at work, etc., and they bring it up often to you, you can actually be causing more harm by listening to them complain! What, you say? How can this be? They need to get this off their chest, don't they? Well, no. What you are doing by listening sympathetically is adding energy to the problem. They feel you "supporting" them when you say, "Yes, that is tough." And their ego is looking for that kind of support. You aren't necessarily meaning to do this, but it is happening. The better response would be to gently refuse to listen to the problems and complaints; instead ask, "What are you going to do about it?" Don't listen to anything else except their active plan to change the situation. *The energy then moves to result, and action, not talking.* Most of us were not taught that valuable lesson growing up. We often see ourselves as good listeners who help others vent and release their frustrations, but it doesn't work quite that way. Action, actual plans, not theories, not anger, not revenge, are better ways to help. Action will lead to a resolution; piling problems and words on top of each other will not. That only increases the wrong kind of energy. Ego loves that. Look for ways to solve the problem and then follow through!

Do! Or Do Not! Ego Doesn't Like Decisions!

Does your ego like living in the present *or* worrying about the past and future? Ego is afraid of the present and cannot operate in the now. If you are fully focused on what you are doing at any moment, ego has no control over you. It moved to the background and for the time being you are free! Think about the last time you were very busy, occupied at work or on a project. Your mind was focused on the situation at hand; ego had a difficult time sticking its nose in, unless you were upset at the time and complaining. Stay neutral, or better yet, positive. It is important for the ego to cause worry about the past and anxiety about the future. This keeps the mind occupied and upset, exactly what ego wants. Ego diminishes when we are living in the present. I am seeing this personally. Often, concepts are just that—concepts—and are not utilized or living in our daily lives, but this one is now becoming active in my own life. I see friends and acquaintances that live in the chosen "worry of the future" and "what might happen" syndrome. They can do little or nothing about it, but this doesn't slow down their angst about what is coming down the pipe. I may have been that way myself, but never terribly so, and much less now. At any given moment I try to see where I am and what I need to do, or what I *actually can do*, and tell myself that that is enough. For right now, that is enough. No more. If I am driving my car across town can I do anything about global warming, much less making sure my son is studying for his college test in algebra? Nope. I can only drive. I can think about driving carefully, and I can use the time to take a quick inventory of what I need to get done in the next time span (day, week, hour?) and when I'm up to date I can let it go, trusting my higher self to remind me when necessary. But right now I am driving and only driving. This is where we get caught up. We try to do too many things at once. There is no such thing as multitasking, not really. If we have three or four things going on, we still concentrate on one at a time, though we may be switching back and forth often. Still it is one at a time. At least our concentration is focused on one. We can walk and chew gum (some of us, anyway) at the same time, but those things need little concentration. The focus may be on the walking, but the gum is below conscious level. It is the focus that matters. If we are not thinking about walking, we actually miss the trip itself. We are suddenly there. We have no real concept of the journey to get there. We have missed a moment of life.

Another topic that has been floating around my mind the last couple days is the phrase "Do. Or do not." This could also be said as, "Do. Or not do." This sums up the basic human response to virtually everything. I've been wondering about the value of talk. How does talk fit in? In this world talk is often called "cheap" and is looked on at being of little value in the scheme of things. Often I would have to agree. Many times we talk about something or other but do little or nothing about it. Maybe there is nothing to be done, naturally, but almost always something *can* be done in some way. That is where I want to shout "Do! Or Do Not!" Those are the choices. Talking on and on about what you are going to do may be necessary for a time to build up the courage, or to get organized to make an actual move, but then to remain inactive, yet want to talk on and on, and when the topic and pros and cons are repeated over and over it is time to Do or Do Not! There comes a point when those around you are fatigued by the talk and discussions that lead nowhere. Do. Or Do Not. One or the other, stop living in between! Those are the possibilities. It is very freeing to make the first steps. Once an action or thought is put into movement, it draws in more energy, and often when the task is completed we wonder why we waited (and talked about it) for so long! We hesitate, stall, and wait just a bit longer for something to change. We say we need certain conditions to line up properly and then we can make the move. We can also wait forever. No, we shouldn't jump into some crazy scheme that uproots everything in our lives without proper preparation, but when the preparation goes on and on and on for months, or years, well, time to do not! Drop it; your ego wants you to keep toying with something you will never do, unless for some reason or another you are forced into action. Of course, if you make up your mind to drop it, the ego will look for other fears and worries to torment you with. It becomes time to examine truthfully whether we will make a change or not. This can only be accomplished by going into Spirit and out of ego. Ego wants us to stay static and continue to do nothing, yet worry, worry, worry. Deciding one way or the other can reduce or eliminate the egoic worry. Do. Or do not. Simple? Yes and no. Difficult? Sometimes. If you truly live in the present, it becomes easier.

In conclusion about ego and Spirit the magic word is, as always, awareness. When you notice your ego at work, you have begun to move away from it. You are reducing its control over you. Let's say you are having a conversation with someone and they tell a story about snorkeling in Hawaii on vacation. Great story, but then you have to tell about the time you went to Hawaii and went to the active volcano, and did the zipline in the rain forest and on and on. You had to top their story. Is this necessary? Ego. If you just said that you had gone there, too, and loved it, well, that would suffice. By trying to top them you are giving into your ego's need to be top dog, number one. Ego lives by comparing everything; your car to theirs, your hairstyle to her hairstyle, your new coat, your office, your kids, everything. Comparisons are egoic exercises, beloved by egos everywhere! When you have to be on top and win at all costs, you have ego run amuck. As you recognize what ego is up to in yourself and others, you become aware, and awareness leads to change. Spirit will lead you away from this kind of no-win thinking. There will always be someone or something better, and your ego will never be satisfied. In fact, that is one of ego's favorites: never being satisfied. There is always something out there newer, shinier, bigger, faster, and you "need" it. This is because we often identify ourselves with what we have, or our job, or our money, or our accomplishments. Ego uses those. How much better would it be if we truly didn't care to evaluate anything in comparison to others? If we accepted life as is? If we dropped all the angst caused by keeping up with the Joneses? Wow, what a thought. Freedom.

It is kind of like this: *If* I only had this certain job I would be happy! Then when you have the job, after a short time: *If* I only had this kind of car, well, then I would be there. But then there is another, better car. *If* I only had this perfect wife or husband, then ... and on and on it goes. Ego is never satisfied, and if you choose to live in the egoic world you will never be satisfied, either. The opposite is acceptance. Accept who you are, where you are, what you do, all in the present moment. No, you don't have to stay in that job, that house, etc., you deserve whatever you want, but putting so much emphasis on those items takes away from your real self. Don't put thought and energy into the negative job, or small house, or unhappy relationship! Put thought and energy into changing it! Go for it with confidence and positive energy. That is how things get done, not by wishing. Bypass ego and become a positive Spiritual person. All things will come to you. Just stop putting the wrong energy to the pursuit. Action fulfills, not whining or words or complaints! Action. Do something about it, and the wise friend will refuse to talk ad nauseum with you about it. They will tell you to actually do something!

TIME

This leads to a few thoughts on time, as we understand it as physical beings on Earth. In the last paragraph I said this moment is all you have. That can't be stated enough to help form an understanding of Spirit. Right now is the only time you have. Many people think about the past, or about the future, and in some cases the past becomes such a powerful focal point for their lives that they miss the present. It is called "living in the past" and it is not uncommon. Then there are those who wish to concentrate on the future. Save money for later, put off things now for the future. Be prepared! The focus is always on later, not now. Anything can happen and we must prepare. Think of every possible issue that could come up and be ready for it. This focus on the future also robs us of the present moment, and if you think about it you realize the "future" never actually gets here, because when it does it is now again, the present moment. So, the idea of living in the moment is perfect. Worrying about something that isn't happening right now is a waste of energy that can be focused in better ways. You can worry about it when it arrives.

WHERE IS LOVE?

If there is a purpose for this book what would it be? Hopefully it has been answered somewhat in the reading. But in retrospect let me put it this way: as we incarnate into human form and live on this Earth we agree to have a sort of amnesia and hide our true natures from ourselves. Most of us do not recall who we really are, that we are Spiritual beings inhabiting human bodies temporarily. OK, and where does that leave us? It leaves us with an understanding of how the universe is balanced and how we can help move the world along in a positive fashion. As we discover there is more to life than what our senses show us, our lives become enriched with meaning and direction. Having a higher goal to reach for removes much of the lower-level concerns. We begin to see others as part of us, each a branch from the tree of humanity. Moving more into a Spiritual frame of reference shows us the folly of judgment. We are one team, all of us. Those who remember or sense the Spiritual aspects of existence assume the leadership roles, and through love and example they affect the world as Jesus did. His life was a perfect example of what life should be. There is no room for hatred, jealousy, or anger, and if those arise we can look them in the eye and see that they are aimed at ourselves. We are judging ourselves when we don't like something about another person. We can replace that judgment with love. Love of others also is love of self. And that is where we start. We cannot share what we do not have, and if we don't love ourselves we can't truly love others. Start with self. Spiritual writer Louise Hay suggests we begin each day with a positive affirmation. Look into the mirror and tell the person you see there, "I love you! You are a perfect person, put on this Earth to nurture love for all." Feel gratitude for everything. Focus on the moment, always the present moment. Do not get bogged down with past memories. The past is gone. The future is not here, nor will it ever be here. We only have the present. Live in it and enjoy it every moment. There is nothing like the grandeur of life on Earth. Yes, we are here to learn, and sometimes learning is difficult, but we are also here to share the abundance of love that has no end! When we make love the focus, the difficult learning becomes less a chore and we see it as an opportunity. To give back, to help, to be of service is what living is all about.

None of us is perfect. But we can become perfect, one step at a time. Becoming aware of Spirit and the truth is step number one. Awareness, Awakening, Remembering, these are all the same, just different terms, and there are many more. If you are feeling that there is "something happening here. What it is ain't exactly clear," to quote the Buffalo Springfield song from the 1960s, then you are not alone, and maybe you are feeling some of what I've covered in this book. This is the beginning of a life rich with possibility and hope. It leads to a change in perspective, a change in attitude, and the effect on those around you can be profound. Changes can be subtle as well. When you become aware, you start noticing small things. Signs and communications that you've ignored your whole life now take on meaning. There are connections; there is much happening at the soul level that starts to sift down to our human consciousness.

THE SPACE BETWEEN

As we begin to awaken we become aware of what I call the "space between." The "place" we can go if we are relaxed and in the moment. Not totally in the physical world, yet not totally in the Spirit world, either. I guess it would be in between, but in order to enter we must, as always, acknowledge the ego and move past the ego's control. It is not a battle so much, but rather a recognition of the role the ego plays in our lives, but there is a downside, too. If the ego gains too much control, we become egocentric and allow little or no room for Spirit. Our lives will be filled with suffering. It doesn't matter if we are rich or poor, what color we are, where we live, etc., if ego rules we suffer, and that is how ego remains in control, by keeping us in various degrees of pain and worry. If we can recognize this and observe it and move past it, we can have joyful, fulfilling lives alongside a diminished ego.

CHAPTER 9

PULLING IT ALL TOGETHER

Wow, that's a lot to take in in the previous eight chapters, isn't it? Now is the time to bring it all together and give you a glimpse of where we are all headed and how you can use this information to help you not only understand the Spiritual changes you and so many others are undergoing, but also how to shape your life in accordance to your own, distinctly *individual* Spiritual path. Great happiness and fulfillment is available to each and every one of us, and by aligning with our chosen path and the goals we've set for ourselves this time around we can truly enjoy life on Earth. In fact, truth be known, we *should* live a life of joy and wonder! It is ours for the taking, just a matter of energy, attitude, and awakening. If you've found and read this book you have probably felt the stirrings of Spiritual awakening, or you are interested, anyway, and awareness is the first step. So many of us have felt a little "different" for many years and didn't quite know why. Society, which overall is ego driven, has provided no words or terms, or even anyone to talk to about this "knowing" that we sometimes experience. This feeling that there is more to it than what we've been led to believe, and that we should have the opportunity to think for ourselves, to learn and grasp amazing things without needing another person to feed it to us. To limit us, which may be the biggest sin of all. We are unlimited beings, and there are no boundaries. We inhabit these bodies for a short time and use that time to learn and grow. When we begin to change our outlook about everything, everything around us changes; there are new meanings, new ideas, and new connections. The overall feeling of Spirit provides a sense of coming home, of getting back to what we knew all along, but were often not allowed to express or were not supported when we tried. We've found out that much of the egoic world is and has been misguided. Money, power, and all the trappings do not provide the fulfillment we had hoped for. There is nothing wrong with any of them, depending on how they are used, of course, but by themselves they provide a shallow dream.

What has been missing is a sense of unity, of oneness with the universe, or more closely, with life around us. That unity is our natural state and should be experienced all the time, not just on Sunday or for brief moments. Breaking away from the egocentric thinking patterns of much of the world takes time and work. There are an amazing number of people awakening to Spirit at this time in our history. All around us the pull is being felt. Some of our closest friends are awakening right now and those who may be a little farther along the path are there to help them, as this book is here to help you, as I and countless others are here to help you. It has been said that there are many of us, and you may be one, who are sometimes called "Lightworkers." The advance group sent to prepare the world for the Spiritual awakening that has started. The label may not be important but the concept is. We need to be ready, to continue to prepare, and share with those who are interested. And believe me, there are many who are interested. They will come to you when you don't expect it and ask if you know anything about psychics or wonder why they dreamed about a long-passed relative, or maybe they just start talking and it leads to some of these kinds of discussions. This will happen more and more as people continue to find Spirit. This is the natural progression and state for all of us. The egoic world has tried to make us believe that the Spiritual approach to life is wrong, that life is built on good and evil, and we will be punished by an angry God for our sins. I don't believe in an angry God. God is love, and love does not punish. Ever.

The world as it is does not satisfy our deepest human desires. We think we need many things, but in truth, the chief soul-level desire we have is for LOVE. And Spirit is love in its purest form. Spirit is God. God is the Essence, the All, the Source. God is One, no matter what name you use. So many religions, yet it is the same God/Spirit/Source. We want Spirit in our lives; in fact, we want Spirit/Love as the central part of our lives, and it can be so. It has always been this way, but so often we give in to the egoic desires surrounding us as humans. We buy into the chase for power over others, the need for great fortunes of money and possessions. Of course none of those so-called needs are of any value when we pass away from this dimension. No value whatsoever! The ego wants us to believe that we have one chance on this planet, and we need to get everything we can while we can, usually at the expense of others. History is full of this kind of thinking. But once you start to feel Spirit in your life, you see the fallacy in that reasoning.

HAPPINESS

True fulfillment and happiness are not built on Earth, but within Spirit. When you begin to awaken you start asking questions, no longer willing to just accept what you are told. Young people of today really are struggling with this. They know intuitively that the old paradigm is off kilter; they have a hard time with what they are being told by an egoic world. So they search, looking for the truth, looking for what they know is right. The old world feels wrong, and they are not satisfied with it. Along with those of us awakening to Spirit at this time they will lead the changing of the world into what it is meant to be. This will take time, and will only be accomplished if we tune into our true paths. Our paths will then begin to work in unison, and we'll be pleasantly surprised to find out we are not alone. There are so many with us, and the focus is simply to love one another, to see we are not separate individuals in competition, but parts of a whole with a unified goal. We want to return to our true home, with our lessons learned, and make this planet and the universe a better place for all.

There will be difficulties. The old paradigm will not go away easily; many will fight for status quo. The egocentric world of capitalism and the philosophy of greed so prevalent in today's world will do everything to keep things as they are. They are mistakenly identifying with the ego's need for more, more, more, and of course they are never satisfied. Keep in mind that we can't change them, we can *only* change ourselves. Focus inward and become an example for others to see and the change we desire will come to us.

This all starts easily, when we begin to become aware. Aware of the true world out there, beyond what our senses tell us. Deep within us, at the soul level, we know. As humans we can't quite grasp it at times, but believe me, we know. We know who we really are as we start to remember. Once we are aware of the truth, we can begin to really dig in and understand it, build our beliefs, and learn to use our talents to find true happiness. Small setbacks will not slow us down. We will see through the egoic patterns that rule so much of the world and ourselves. When we see things for how they really are, our view changes.

What should you do, the reader of this book? First of all, don't worry or sweat it. If it is your time to wake up to Spirit you will feel an interest begin deep inside, and you will find yourself drawn to some of this information. It will just feel right to you. You may not understand much of it, even, but you sense there is something there and that it might hold some answers. Your path has been sighted. If none of this feels right or resonates, you are simply at a different point on your path. There are no rights or wrongs, just a feeling of what is right for you. There are many paths back home, and it will become more obvious as more people wake up to Spirit that they are to become the leaders and helpers for the future. It is entirely possible you are one of them.

MANIFESTING YOUR OWN REALITY

Perceptions of reality. Key phrase. High importance. Where the rubber hits the road. One's reality is controlled by one's perception of that reality. We choose whether our reality is "for us" or "against us," and the evidence comes after we decide. So, you choose to feel badly about life, you have headaches all the time, you are tired, you don't sleep well, you don't have much money, you hate your job. Well, those attitudes and views are your reality and will continue to grow stronger. Others who choose a happier reality of abundance and happiness will not want to be around you. If they feel your reality is lacking or damaged or negative they will not want to come around because this drains their energy and they feel beaten down just by being around you! "I have no friends!" Yep, if you say that enough watch what happens, you won't have any friends! Manifests. All you really have and can control is your perception of reality and that is in your power to form and create. Being unhappy with your reality can lead to blame, and once you conveniently place the problem "out there" and give up ownership you can continue to feel terrible through "no fault of your own!" It is their fault! Or circumstances! Or fate! It's anything but your own fault. And so the circle continues until it is broken. Once you understand that your reality is really up to you to create and no one else is in charge, you can then take steps to move in a more positive direction. The focus on positive brings more positive.

I'm not talking about other's realities, though you can have an impact on them as a teacher, guide, or leader. Leading by example is very powerful. You cannot control even your own children's realities; only ego would even think you could. Their reality can be influenced by you, but again, not controlled. Doesn't work that way. The very best anyone can do is decide that they want a life of abundance, happiness, and opportunities to learn and grow. Notice I said *decide*. There is no other way. Can you get up one morning and say that you are going to be positive and manifest only good things into your life? Yes, you can. Will you be successful the first time? Why not? The old thought patterns created by ego will fight back and do everything possible to take control and drag you down. Back to "Woe is me! Nothing ever goes right for me! I never get a break!" Think about those words. What if you had the magical power to make the words you say and think become your reality? This sounds crazy but that is the *actual, absolute truth*. Think positive, manifest positive. Simple.

How do we think and manifest in a positive direction? Well, breaking it down to the lowest levels, when you wake up feeling crabby and tired and grouchy and start thinking that today is going to be a terrible day, well, bingo! Yes, it will be. If you realize that you are doing that, you are halfway home! The realization that you are undermining the good energy that is available for you to tap into will start the change, if you really want change, that is. Let's say you would like to move in a more positive, fulfilling direction. You now recognize that you are manifesting unhappy occurrences, and you can begin the change to more positive outcomes. Whenever a thought of doom and gloom sneaks in, recognize it, gently look at it, and think of a positive response to the situation and how you can act on it. Then do it! Act on it at the first chance you get. It may be something very small. "I'm so tired I need to take a nap when I get home from work." "I'm so tired because I didn't sleep well in bed last night!" Well, put two and two together. Realize you've created a circle of negative thought and manifestation. You're not sleeping well at night because you've taken a nap too late in the day. You are then tired when you get home from work because you've created an expectation of having a nap. Then you can't sleep well at night, on and on. Once you see this, refuse to take that nap; find something to do. If you still have problems sleeping there may be more at play here. Most important is that you recognize it, decide to do something, and do it! These actions will work together over time to make it your normal mode of operation, and then it gets much easier. Start thinking in a positive direction for everything negative that comes in. Find the other side and do something about it. These add up. Sitting still and wishing, or worse, complaining, continues the cycle in the wrong direction.

The key is that we do create our own reality and we choose how we will react to everything. These are conscious decisions, and the results are what leads to happiness. Or not. It's up to each one of us to decide.

Maintaining Your Spiritual "Interest"

The following is taken from my journal:

How does a person stay in Spirit or not backtrack when they are opening up? That is a great question. So, let's dig in. There is no doubt that as you begin there is a certain excitement and enthusiasm. But, nothing sustains itself without further energy input. Now, I'm not sure how this works for everyone else, but for me I suspect it is one of two things: my guides and/or my higher self, are supplying me with the needed energy to keep my focus moving forward, OR it is the excellent coffee I'm drinking! No kidding, I seem to want a second cup of coffee whenever I start working in my journal, and then I am basically buzzing. So, is it caffeine, or something higher? Don't know. But I'm smiling at such a dumb question, now I'm actually laughing because it doesn't matter at all. *Energy is available whenever we want or need it, we just have to picture it, ask for it, and there it is.*

Personally, keeping my interest in the Spiritual side of life since my own awakening has been a non-issue; in fact, I have to rein myself in because there is so much to do and think about and experience. I feel like my "real self" has been released and allowed to breathe, in public! Yikes! Or, again, it could be the coffee. This is good coffee. OK, back to the topic: if you feel a strong push from your soul to pursue the esoteric or Spiritual arts or way of life it may sustain itself, just rolls on. But I think the question is more along the lines of, "What if you are not so strongly drawn in, at least on the surface, and find yourself wandering away from this way of thinking?" Good question. The best answer I have is to not worry about it. If you have to force yourself to keep a certain way of thinking it may not be meant for you.

Or you don't need it. It may be just below your conscious level, but humming along just fine. I know someone who is very spiritual, full of love for everyone, who helps everyone she knows. She draws people to her for her kindness, caring attitude, and soothing calmness. She does not need to worry about her Spirituality. She lives it, doesn't have to think about it all the time, in fact, she doesn't actually need to think about it at all; it is her life. She is worried that she might be losing interest, but there is nothing to worry about. She continues to read books and watch videos and discuss these topics but she feels her interest may be waning just a bit and she is concerned. No need to be. That part is fulfilled, now she must just relax and live it, and she is doing that.

But does this work for everyone? Yes. You cannot force yourself to live in Spirit or to read books or go to meetings, etc. Well, you can force yourself, but to what end? You'll gain little or nothing. Your heart and soul will tell you what to do if you listen. So follow the best guide you have, yourself. Learn to tune in and the answers will be there. Don't worry, don't stress, don't think you have to do anything ... besides, I have enough enthusiasm for all of you!

SPIRITUAL HELPERS

Let's go back to the topic of Spirit Guides and angels. This seems to be of great interest and importance. I talk to them and ask for answers, but I believe they work in their own time frame and in their own way. Is it OK to ask for proof or validation? Yes, you can, but be specific so you don't miss the connection and communication. Don't say, "Oh, Spirit Guides, please show me a sign that all is well." OK, you've asked, but you certainly didn't give them any idea of what kind of sign you want, and though you may well get a sign you might miss it. If you ask them to answer in a song, or by showing you a certain kind of bird, or something more specific, you will be less likely to miss it.

Hopefully by journaling about this I can continue to open doors and bring about the changes desired. But how do we deal with doubt? Does it stop you in your tracks? It can hinder results. But it seems like a catch-22 then. Without faith we may block proof and without proof we may not be able to muster faith? Yikes. Then I step back, drink more coffee (see journal entry above) and laugh. Does it even matter? It is what it is and nothing more, so belief and faith and proof don't matter in a way because they will not change anything except our perception of what is "real." Hmmm, something to think about. What is "real" anyway? Next book perhaps.

I am now convinced that we create our own reality and if we believe something is important it will be for us, but if we push it gently aside it will not resonate the same way. So, belief and faith are key to our reality, but we shouldn't get too hung up on the terms. Our Spirit will show us the way and guide us regardless of how much validity we put in words.

TERMS

The following are some terms that resonate with me, and I hope with you, too!

Heaven: This is an often-covered and confusing issue. Is Heaven a place in the clouds we move to upon death? Is it physical? Do we have the brainpower to even know? Can we understand or do we vibrate too slowly to understand? Lots of questions. Some say Heaven is here on Earth; others think it is a magical place where every wish is granted. I think the term Heaven may be used too broadly. Heaven may be the fifth-dimension setting. If this is so, there are a number of higher dimensions after that, so a watered-down Heaven? I'm not sure. But Heaven represents in our culture a place where we can rest, a final place for us, but this is not necessarily the case if other dimensions exist and we are moving that way. So, is Heaven the legendary final dimension, the highest dimension? Or is it a holding pen? And we'll get to it someday? Personally I think Heaven is wherever you are if you are of clear thought, ego off to the side, and if you've reached some part of enlightenment or Spirit in your life. Not a place, a state of mind. That's what I think, anyway.

Hope: This cannot be undervalued. Hope makes even the most difficult situation and circumstances tolerable, because hope indicates there is a possibility for positive change. Without hope: depression, fear, pain, and worry: hope-less-ness. Hope also motivates you to take the needed steps to alleviate what is bothering you. Without hope changes must be forced on you from the outside, but with hope you can find the motivation to change from within. Even the most dire life setting can be tolerated if there is hope. This is what we are bringing to each other as we awaken: Hope.

Goals: Why did I include this? Because it gives us direction. It motivates us to stay on our path, to follow through. Hope will lead to goals. Goals are needed to move us forward. Doesn't matter how small or large the goals are. With right-mindedness (the Buddha), we can reach those goals. Nothing is truly out of reach. Goals can be specific or broad. "Staying on the right path" is a broad goal, while "changing my job" is more specific. All goals are changeable and fluid, but they are a must to get things moving. If we realize that a goal we have set no longer fits our needs, we simply drop it or change it. A new goal will be just as pertinent. Always guard for ego interference, however. If the time comes that we must drop a goal, the ego may happily leap in with the thoughts of FAILURE! LOSER! And more. It will try to show us we can't do it, we cannot reach our goals. Do not fall for this! Know your ego and know the tricks the ego will use to get you off balance and unhappy. Note the "concerns" of the ego and release them, trusting your true self (soul-self) to help you find your correct goal(s) and that the guidance and help you need to get there will be made available when needed.

Butterfly Feelings in the Stomach: Oh yes. I feel this all the time when I think I'm getting nearer to something amazing or magical. When I'm meditating and feeling change I can get this feeling pretty strongly. I had wondered about this because I thought my being scared or nervous or not ready for the changes I was sensing caused it. But I had my feelings of nervous stomach validated at a seminar when the presenter mentioned that that exact feeling is a strong indicator that angels and guides are present and trying to connect with you! This was a big relief, because I thought maybe I would never get past this feeling and that it reflected an unready person (me). So, I will embrace this feeling when it pops up and hope that it truly is the way he says. Makes me feel better about it, that's for sure.

Validation: The KING of all words when you are starting out in the journey of self is *validation*. When you begin to awaken to the true path, you have many doubts, much confusion, frightening moments, and begin to question yourself a great deal because this is a bit of an about-face for many, at least in our culture. When we receive personal validation or an insight, intuitive feeling, or just know something, it confirms what our higher self is telling us. It lets us know that we are on the right track; we are headed in the correct direction. Validation confirms what we sense rather than know in the usual ways, and as validation grows stronger we no longer have to look for it or desire it as much because we do know. Truth be told, I don't think anyone ever grows out of needing validation, though it will take on different, changing levels for each person. As we get to know our true selves, we learn to trust, and validation is not needed as much as before. In the beginning, however, it is the difference between moving on and giving up. We no longer are willing to take someone else's word for what is what, what is real, or how to interpret signs and messages. We can do it with validation at the right time and of the right kind.

CHAPTER 10

SOME FINAL THOUGHTS

If in the long run you are saying, "So what?" you would not be at fault. That is a perfectly acceptable response to all of this, actually. Most people on the Earth are growing up without exposure to Spiritual thinking along these lines and they are doing fine. The reasons you have read this book and found yourself interested in this subject matter is because you were meant to be involved, possibly by yourself, but maybe with others as well. Strength in the world of Spirit is enhanced tremendously when working with like-minded people. If you find yourself needing more proof or simply wanting to feel a part of it, look deeply into your own soul, through meditation, and see the connections provided. They are there and you will find them if it is your path. Again, if you find you have no interest, that is OK. You can follow your own way; the formal path is not needed. Everyday life is full of Spirit and it is simply the way we are, and each and every thought and action is connected to Spirit. How strongly you feel it and act on it is up to you.

I feel like I should include a bit more information about why I wrote this book. Here is how it happened. I had a meeting with an amazing psychic here in Omaha, Nebraska, recently, and she suggested that I keep a journal, which I mentioned earlier in the book. That journal really took off and I found I was typing pages up very quickly, and often the information was not something I knew much about. I actually had to go back and read the journal entries to see what came out. This of course shocked me, and some friends explained that I was channeling my Spirit Guides. The ideas that came through popped into my head as I typed and I didn't know what the next word, phrase, or sentence might be,

I just typed. The journal, which continues to this day, provided clarification and helped me develop a picture of the human/Spirit duality. After a while I began to type up questions for my Spirit Guides and the answers came through right away. Selections from the journal are available on my Spiritual website: http://www.wakinguptospirit.com.

This book, however, is not from the journal, other than one passage earlier in this chapter, though many of the ideas originally developed in the journal writing. I had thought to release entries from the journal as a book, but decided to create something new. The content is of great importance to me, and hopefully to others, though it is aimed at newly awakening folks who simply want some straight-talk answers. We all live in a Spiritual world, but over the centuries we have been moving away from recognizing it. We have become focused on money, power, and possessions. These are all temporary. Only the soul/Spirit lasts forever. The good news is that humanity's focus is beginning to flip back to Spirit as more and more awaken. I'm one, and so many of my closest friends are, too. If you are reading this you are also most likely feeling the call; the call beyond the physical world we are so immersed in. Many of us are starting to see, hear, sense, and feel the signs of Spirit as I've described in the earlier chapters. We are becoming aware of the connections, that what we do unto others we truly do unto ourselves. We are related at a much stronger level than we ever realized, we are actually one with each and every other person, all parts of God. As we internalize these ideas, our lives change. And it is a wonderful, fulfilling change. Life has meaning again apart from work, work, work; money, money, money; power, power, power. This new focus allows us to see beyond the physical shell of the person standing in front of us. We see into their soul; we recognize ourselves within others; we know that we are connected and that we are all together in this learning process. The playing field is leveled; no one is more important or less important than anyone else. Our lessons while on Earth become easier to understand.

Very young children are strongly connected with the Spirit world that for most of us is just beyond our grasp. They have not lost the connection, yet. Have you seen a baby suddenly look off or up into space and start giggling or outright laughing? They are seeing what most of us cannot, but this can change as we awaken. We all had this natural connection as babies, but often our lessons on Earth won't be as fruitful if we remember our true nature, so the connection with Spirit fades from our human memories. The veil can be lifted. There is no hurry, however. We are perfect in each and every moment, and life will move along, as it should. The difference is in the level of interest we develop and how we want to learn. Others may be doubtful, skeptical, and even downright irate! But we don't have to be loud about it. We are called to work within, to connect on our own, and as we do we will discover like-minded people are all around! It is amazing; there will be a cadre of new friends just waiting to meet you, if you are sincere. As always, be aware of ego, and the desire to be "more Spiritual" than others. It is not a competition. Only ego competes. Recognizing who we really are removes any need for competing.

When I felt the strong pull of awakening in the last couple of years, I knew something important had happened. I met many others who felt the same way, including friends I'd known for a very long time. What I did not know is that they too were searching and finding the same answers. Wonderful, but the best part was when we got together and compared notes. A new bond was developed that was stronger than ever, a bond that continues today.

As we open up to Spirit we will find ourselves looking back at our lifetime, and at the important decisions we made, the mistakes, strokes of luck, and the pain, sorrow, and love we experienced. The past is seen in a different light. We begin to understand why we chose to do certain things, why we went along with some crazy ideas and why we said no to others. There are reasons behind our life's ups and downs, and they begin to make sense. Best of all, we can get beyond the pain with understanding and realize the past is gone. We only have now, and each now moment is a fresh start. We can choose to do whatever we want to do at this moment! There is no need to dwell on *what happened before*, no need to worry about *what is coming up in the future*. We only have the *now of this moment*. Followed by the now of the next moment, but always right now only. Thinking about and living in either the past or the future serves no purpose; in fact, they both take away from what we do have, this moment. Yes, we put some time in to prepare for the future, but we don't constantly live in it that preparation. Same for what has happened in the past. We learn lessons, we cherish memories, we laugh at all the silly things we did, but we don't live there. We only have this moment. It sounds complicated, but it is so basic and important to be present. That is what makes life full and rewarding.

Where do I go from here? My psychic friend has told me there will be more books, travel, and happiness. I hope so. There is a great deal of content not covered in this book. But we have begun the journey, you and I, and I expect it to pick up speed as we move along. There seems to be a vast movement toward a happier Spiritual existence in our world. The old ways are beginning to crumble, and we are here at the right time.

So keep your eyes open, accept what you feel, ask your own Spirit Guides to help you along, to give you signs and watch over you. It may seem selfish, but it is not. You must take care of yourself before you can help others, physically, emotionally, and Spiritually. You can focus on yourself in your Spiritual growth, and this will impact those around you. It starts in your heart and spreads from there. I look forward to the new world we are all creating, and now is the time to begin the journey. We are all in this together. We are all part of the same Spirit, and when we remove the ego's influence we can see clearly that everyone is as beautiful and worthwhile and important as every other person. When we feel this in our hearts we truly see others differently, and it is a wonderful way to go through this human existence.

Finally, this book offers little advice on how to get to where you are going Spiritually. It is meant to offer some glimpses of Spiritual thinking, and help you see Spirit in everyday life. The real journey is within, and from there it expands. Trust yourself, trust your Spirit Guides, and trust God. You will not be led astray. You will find yourself.

THE MAN IN THE MOUNTAIN GOES HOME

There once was a man who lived in the mountains. He saw people rarely in his life. He wasn't usually lonely, though. He was at peace and felt love all around him. He never really felt alone. When people would come see him in the mountains he found he had little in common with them, but he treated them kindly and welcomed them. He was not sorry to see them leave, though. The man spent a lot of time thinking, but he spent even more time not thinking, and let his mind be still. This pleased him and he felt it was the right thing to do. He didn't have the terms for this, and didn't understand it, but he knew how he felt.

One day he heard a scratching at the front door of his cabin. He didn't know what to expect, but he went to the door, opened it, and saw a small raccoon. The animal looked healthy and seemed unafraid and yet somehow lost. Not yet fully grown, the little creature quietly walked into the cabin. This surprised the man a little, but he was not overly concerned. It had turned chilly outside with the coming of autumn, and he was glad to have a little company. The raccoon didn't appear to need anything; it just looked around curiously, then went to the fireplace, curled up, and fell asleep on the woven rug in front. This was unusual, thought the man, yet he wasn't concerned because the raccoon seemed like a peaceful little fellow. So, while the raccoon slept the man made some supper for himself and then realized his guest would be hungry when waking from his nap, so he went out back of the cabin and retrieved a couple cobs of corn left over from his summer crop. The kernels were dry and hard, but he thought it would be all right. Sure enough, a couple hours passed by and the little bandit-faced visitor woke up, yawned, stretched, blinked his eyes a couple of times, and looked around. The man placed a small bowl of clean water nearby and a second bowl of corn next to it. The little fellow looked at him and waddled over to the bowls. He dipped his front paws into the water and washed them in his fashion. He then sniffed the corn and began to eat. He was very hungry after all and cleared the bowl out quickly, and enjoyed a long drink of the cold water. After a couple more minutes of cleaning up, he looked around and went to the door. The man got up from his chair, and still, without fear, moved to the door. As it swung open the visitor slipped out into the darkness. The man felt a little sad. His new friend was around for such a short time! And he had a friendly face, and he even picked up the corn like he had tiny human-like hands. He wondered if he would see the raccoon again, or if this was just a quick visit in the night? He was surprised that a wild animal would seem so fearless; after all, the man was over six feet tall, with a long gray beard and flowing hair. He hadn't seen a mirror for many years, but figured he was probably a frightening site. But the little friend had had no fear of him; he seemed to sense that he was safe.

The day went by and it was time for bed. The man went outside and looked around, maybe hoping a little face would appear and come back in, but he was nowhere to be found. So, giving up, with a sigh he went on to his bed and settled in. During the night, might have been a few hours later, he felt something by his legs. Small. Warm. Fuzzy! And lightly snoring! The man woke up fully but didn't move. He wasn't sure what to do. He was sure it was the little bandit, but when did he come back? How did he get in? Why didn't the man hear him? How could this be? So he thought for a while, but still didn't move. Was he safe with this wild creature lying next to him? He didn't feel any fear, just a soft warmness. So, he looked around the dark cabin, said a prayer to his ancestors and found himself relaxing and falling back to sleep. He still couldn't figure out how the raccoon had gotten into the cabin, and what about others? This was a very young fellow, but wouldn't he have siblings and parents somewhere close? He didn't know. Well, these things would just have to sort themselves out in the morning. For the first time in a long time he felt another life connected with him and it woke something up in his heart. Sleep found him and when he awoke the sun was coming up.

He looked around. No raccoon. Where had he gone? He got up, looked under the bed, behind the boxes in the corner, everywhere in his little cabin. Nothing. That was strange. The door was shut, wasn't it? He checked and realized that for some reason the night before he had not latched the leather loop over the nail to hold the door shut! He never forgot that! Then he wondered if he did that so the door would swing in easily, just in case someone wanted in? Could it be? Had the little creature connected with him in some unspoken way that would cause him to leave the door unhooked? He was puzzled, but also somewhat happy, yet now lonely. What was going on here? He had not felt lonely for years, so what was this? He opened the door and the sunshine felt warm and surprisingly bright on his small porch. And sitting quietly gazing out at the sun was his little friend greeting the morning. The raccoon turned and looked at the man. But didn't move away, so the man walked over to the steps, sat down close to the little fellow and looked out at the morning with him. They sat quietly for a while, with no stress, no fear, and no hurry, just accepting. But after awhile, the man realized his guest must be hungry again, so he carefully got up, but then he changed his mind and sat back down. He slowly reached his hand out to the raccoon who continued to look out at the valley as the sun rose higher. He touched the little furry creature on the back, very gently. The raccoon gave a small start and turned to look at the man, but then settled down. So the man very lightly ran his finger down the raccoon's back and after a couple times the raccoon relaxed. There was no fear. The man was quite surprised how this seemed to be the right thing to do. He had never touched a raccoon in his life, never had a dog or a cat. This was strange, but it seemed OK. After a bit he again thought about food, so got up slowly and entered the cabin.

After a few seconds, one mystery was solved. The little hands and face pushed open the door a few inches, he didn't need much room to squeeze in, and walked over to where the man was, sat down on the floor, and looked up at him, and the man swore that that little raccoon smiled and winked! If anything could make the man laugh, this was just the thing, and he started giggling and guffawing and belly laughing to see such a comical face looking at him! And the little raccoon fell over, and rolled over a couple of times, as if joining in the mirth. But all things come to an end, and after all, they were both still hungry, so the man wiped his eyes, having enjoyed himself more in the last few minutes than he had in years, and prepared water and corn for his guest, as well as his own breakfast. They ate in comfortable silence, and the man wondered if this creature was going to stay with him. As he looked down he thought to himself that he sure hoped so. He felt something new stirring within him, something long gone, from way back as a child. But he didn't want to put words to it; it was magic, and words might destroy what was happening. So he just stayed present in the moment and let things move as they would. Soon they finished their breakfast, and after cleaning up they decided to go back outside in the sunshine again.

There were tall weeds growing by the path from the cabin down to the stream where the man got his water every day, and he had planned on trimming them down a bit to make the walk easier. At first he thought he would skip it and wait a day or so, but after a bit decided to go ahead and get it done. Even with a visitor he had things he had to do, so he went to his little shed in the back of the cabin, got out his corn knife, and walked back to the path. He didn't see his new friend, but thought to himself that he is a wild creature and must be allowed to come and go as he pleased. He set to work, moving slowly along working the left side first and then coming back up the path a few paces at a time and trimming the right side. When both sides were trimmed the path was about three feet wide, which offered plenty of room for carrying his jug and pail to the water without getting stickers and brambles on his arms and sleeves. In a couple of hours, he was done and looked over his work. Satisfied, he walked back up the path and around to the shed. No sign of his new friend, and he hoped he hadn't left for good.

The rest of the day went by, and he began to wonder if the little raccoon had gone away. He had no idea how a wild animal thinks, or how it makes decisions, but he suspected there was more going on than it seemed. He wondered if they simply lived minute to minute like he did. If so, there may be no real pattern or plan to the raccoon's whereabouts. He may be a wanderer from day to day. He supposed this was possible, so he tried to move on through his day as always. Finally, he went to bed and felt again surprisingly lonely. How could a little animal make him feel this way? This was something long dead and buried. He didn't need anyone else, and no one needed him! But still, an empty ache lived in his belly tonight. This was different. And he had no answer. So he tried to sleep. Eventually he was able to do just that, and sadly drifted off. After a bit he jumped up! He ran to the door and opened it. Nothing. The wind. But this time he made sure he didn't hook the door shut as he had before, just in case.

Morning. A furry lump by his legs. What? When? How did? He was confused; he hadn't heard or felt anything during the night. In fact, he thought he had slept badly and seemed awake most of the night. How did the little bandit get in and up on the bed without him knowing? He hated to move, to awaken his little friend, but he did reach down to gently run his finger down the raccoon's back again. The creature moved slightly, but was so tired he didn't seem to wake up. Feeling braver, the man rubbed his finger between the raccoon's ears and neck, and the little visitor stretched and yawned, and obviously enjoyed the petting. So the man continued until the raccoon rolled over on his back as though he wanted his tummy rubbed. And the man did just that, when suddenly the raccoon's arms reached out and grabbed the man's hand, pulling it in, and his teeth flashed out as though to bite. But the little raccoon's teeth touched his hand and stopped. No bite. A little lick. Another. He looked up with those large bandit eyes right into the man's eyes and gave him another lick with his tiny tongue. Then he let go. The man withdrew his hand in amazement. He hadn't been bitten. After all, this was a wild animal living in the mountains. But instead of questioning and wondering, the man simply accepted. He didn't need a reason; things just were as they were. So he smiled and his little friend winked again.

So they settled into a simple life, the raccoon coming and going during the day and sleeping next to the man's legs at night and they became a small family. The man never saw another raccoon so figured this little fellow had been abandoned or had gotten lost. He certainly didn't show any fear of the man and became quite tame. After a couple of months (it was now winter), the little fellow spent more and more time with the man, on his lap when he was reading in his old rocker, or on the bed at night, or down by the fireplace, and the man began to talk to him. And when he talked, the raccoon would look right at him and tilt his head from side to side as if he understood, and the man came to believe that he did understand. Such was their life over the winter.

Now the man was not young, and he was not in the best of health, so it came about one night that as he slept he felt some pain in his chest. He was used to various pains and aches, but this one was a bit more than usual. It woke him up, and he sat up slowly, hoping the pain would go away. His little friend looked at him, and moved closer, climbing onto his lap. This comforted the man, and he did begin to feel a little better. After a time, he lay back down and fell asleep again, now with the little raccoon lying against him near his chest, snuggled in closely. Just before he fell asleep, he had an overwhelming sense of pure love. Was it from the little bandit? Or the universe? It didn't matter, he knew his friend somehow caused the wonderful feeling, so he reached out and put his arm around the little wild animal, and for the first time since he was a small boy a teardrop ran down his face, warm and full of feeling, and like that they went back to sleep.

A while later, he wasn't sure how long, the man had a dream, and in this dream he had no pain at all. The years of aches and soreness were gone! He felt fantastic! He looked around. He was in a large clover field, and some of the blossoms had opened, and he could smell them! He hadn't been able to smell anything for years! So sweet and beautiful! He saw white-capped mountains in the distance, and felt a warm, soft breeze in his hair. What was going on? It was winter, wasn't it? Where was he? He had a moment of panic, and then remembered that this was a dream. Dreams can have lots of good things in them he knew, so he relaxed a bit and wished this dream didn't have to end. Well, might as well enjoy it while I can, he thought, so he looked around some more and took a few steps in the field. His knees no longer ached; he felt light as a feather and had a notion to run through the field. It felt so real! Suddenly he looked over and saw his little bandit friend was also in the dream, smiling up at him! And he walked over, picked up the raccoon, and hugged him. He was rewarded with a wink and a kiss on the nose. The man couldn't help it, dream or no dream, this was fantastic! And he started to laugh, and he swore his little friend laughed with him. And life seemed full and wonderful and beautiful, and he felt so complete and happy since the little bandit was with him. He could feel his friend's thoughts, and they were both so full of life that he set the raccoon down and they started to run in the field. After a while they stopped and found a clear, cold stream. After a drink they lay down on the mossy bank and the man suddenly understood. He told his little friend, "You brought me here, didn't you? I don't think this is dream anymore. You came to get me. All my pain is gone, and I feel great. And I want to stay here, with you, my little friend." The little raccoon looked up and winked.

Epilogue: when springtime came to the mountains some hikers happened upon an old cabin sitting back in the middle of nowhere, and in it they found an elderly man's body. He had obviously passed away some time ago. He seemed so alone up here by himself. But something even stranger was found. A small raccoon was curled up in his arms, and it, too, was dead.

ACKNOWLEDGEMENTS

I wish to thank those who have so profoundly affected me on this journey. Each of us has our own path to follow but those paths are only traveled with the help of many others.

Huge thanks to:

Kathie McCurdy Bird, my wife, for understanding my vision and encouraging me through all of it. She truly "gets" it.

Jodi Jorgensen, for reintroducing me to the world of Spirit and opening up my mind at just the right time.

Dan Palensky, for the long talks we've had over the years that always inspire.

Teresa Paulsen, for encouraging me more than anyone else, and who took to heart what I wrote. Her positive energy kept me going so many times.

Patty Gould, for unlocking the doors and helping us glimpse ourselves as we actually are. I am ever grateful.

Others whom I wish to thank for their ideas, support, and friendship, and who have made such an impact include, but are not limited to Deb Brockmann, Angela and John Pennisi, Gina Hickcox, Andy Myers, Tom Majerus, Carly and Zach Milleson, Molly Bird, Nick Bird, Tom Bird, Tom Kenney, Rick Hillyard, Susan and Bob Carpenter, Steve Bird, Mike Bird, and Alan and Nadine Plambeck.

ABOUT THE AUTHOR

Dr. Dan Bird has been interested in Spiritual topics since he was a teenager. Though raised loosely in a religious community and even attending a parochial school from grades three through twelve, he had questions that were not satisfactorily answered within the views of the church. After many years as a musician, he became a teacher and technology trainer for Nebraska's largest school district. He earned a doctorate in education from the University of Nebraska with a focus on the use of technology in the schools. All the while, the search for the real meaning of life, why we are here, and where are we going continued, leading to the writing of this, his first book.

A prolific songwriter, Dr. Bird has performed over fifty of his own compositions solo, in duets, trios, and even full rock and country bands. His music can be heard at http://danbirdmusic.com.

Married with four grown children, he keeps busy traveling, writing, and adding to his Spiritual webpage: http://wakinguptospirit.com.

He lives with his wife, Kathie, in Omaha, Nebraska.

Other Books By Ozark Mountain Publishing, Inc.

Dolores Cannon
A Soul Remembers Hiroshima
Between Death and Life
Conversations with Nostradamus,
    Volume I, II, III
The Convoluted Universe -Book One,
    Two, Three, Four, Five
The Custodians
Five Lives Remembered
Jesus and the Essenes
Keepers of the Garden
Legacy from the Stars
The Legend of Starcrash
The Search for Hidden Sacred Knowledge
They Walked with Jesus
The Three Waves of Volunteers and the
    New Earth
Aron Abrahamsen
Holiday in Heaven
Out of the Archives – Earth Changes
Justine Alessi & M. E. McMillan
Rebirth of the Oracle
Kathryn/Patrick Andries
Naked In Public
Kathryn Andries
The Big Desire
Dream Doctor
Soul Choices: Six Paths to Find Your Life
    Purpose
Soul Choices: Six Paths to Fulfilling
    Relationships
Patrick Andries
Owners Manual for the Mind
Tom Arbino
You Were Destined to be Together
Rev. Keith Bender
The Despiritualized Church
Dan Bird
Waking Up in the Spiritual Age
O.T. Bonnett, M.D./Greg Satre
Reincarnation: The View from Eternity
What I Learned After Medical School
Why Healing Happens
Julia Cannon
Soul Speak – The Language of Your Body
Ronald Chapman
Seeing True
Albert Cheung
The Emperor's Stargate
Jack Churchward
Lifting the Veil on the Lost Continent of Mu
The Stone Tablets of Mu
Sherri Cortland
Guide Group Fridays
Raising Our Vibrations for the New Age
Spiritual Tool Box
Windows of Opportunity

Cinnamon Crow
Chakra Zodiac Healing Oracle
Teen Oracle
Michael Dennis
Morning Coffee with God
God's Many Mansions
Claire Doyle Beland
Luck Doesn't Happen by Chance
Jodi Felice
The Enchanted Garden
Max Flindt/Otto Binder
Mankind: Children of the Stars
Arun & Sunanda Gandhi
The Forgotten Woman
Maiya & Geoff Gray-Cobb
Angels -The Guardians of Your Destiny
Seeds of the Soul
Carolyn Greer Daly
Opening to Fullness of Spirit
Julia Hanson
Awakening To Your Creation
Donald L. Hicks
The Divinity Factor
Anita Holmes
Twidders
Antoinette Lee Howard
Journey Through Fear
Vara Humphreys
The Science of Knowledge
Victoria Hunt
Kiss the Wind
James H. Kent
Past Life Memories As A Confederate
    Soldier
Mandeep Khera
Why?
Dorothy Leon
Is Jehovah An E.T
Mary Letorney
Discover The Universe Within You
Sture Lönnerstrand
I Have Lived Before
Irene Lucas
Thirty Miracles in Thirty Days
Susan Mack & Natalia Krawetz
My Teachers Wear Fur Coats
Patrick McNamara
Beauty and the Priest
Maureen McGill
Baby It's You
Maureen McGill & Nola Davis
Live From the Other Side
Henry Michaelson
And Jesus Said – A Conversation
Dennis Milner
Kosmos

Other Books By Ozark Mountain Publishing, Inc.

For more information about any of the above titles, soon to be released titles,
or other items in our catalog, write, phone or visit our website:
PO Box 754, Huntsville, AR 72740
479-738-2348/800-935-0045
www.ozarkmt.com